Frederick Douglass
The Black Lion

by Patricia and Fredrick McKissack

 CHILDRENS PRESS®
CHICAGO

DEDICATION

To Moses Andrew McKissack and
the staff of the Frederick Douglass
Early Childhood Center

ACKNOWLEDGMENTS

Quotations of Frederick Douglass from *Life and Times of Frederick Douglass* by Frederick Douglass, copyright © 1962 by Macmillan Publishing Co., Inc. and 1970 Ebony Classic *My Bondage and My Freedom* by Frederick Douglass, copyright © 1970 by Johnson Publishing Company, Inc.

PICTURE ACKNOWLEDGMENTS

Historical Pictures Service, Inc., Chicago—2, 8, 65, 68 (2 photos), 69 (middle and bottom), 70 (bottom), 71 (top), 72 (2 photos), 120
National Park Service, U.S. Department of the Interior—5
North Wind Picture Archives—10, 66 (2 photos), 67 (top), 71 (bottom)
From the collections at the Library of Congress—67 (bottom)
The Kansas State Historical Society, Topeka—69 (top)
Sophia Smith Collection, Smith College, Massachusetts—70 (top)
Cover illustration by Len W. Meents

Library of Congress Cataloging in Publication Data
McKissack, Pat, 1944-
    Frederick Douglass: the black lion.

    Includes index.
    Summary: Describes the life and work of the man who escaped slavery to become an orator, writer, and leader in the anti-slavery movement of the nineteenth century.
    1. Douglass, Frederick, 1817?-1895—Juvenile literature.
2. Abolitionists—United States—Biography—Juvenile literature. 3. Afro-Americans—Biography—Juvenile literature. 4. Slavery—United States—Anti-slavery movements—Juvenile literature.
[1. Douglass, Frederick, 1817?-1895. 2. Abolitionists. 3. Afro-Americans—Biography. 4. Slavery—Anti-slavery movements] I. McKissack, Fredrick. II. Title.
E449.D75M38   1987   973.8′092′4 [B][92]   86-32695
ISBN 0-516-03221-6

    2 3 4 5 6 7 8 9 10 R 96 95 94 93 92 91 90 89 88

Table of Contents

INTRODUCTION

Whenever people gather to discuss freedom, justice, and the rights of mankind, they usually quote Frederick Douglass: "Every man knows that slavery is not right for him. . . ." Who was he, really?

Frederick Douglass was a slave; he was also a caulker by trade, a great antislavery orator, journalist, writer, and United States consul general and minister resident to Haiti under President Harrison. These are impressive credentials. But, what was he like, really?

One poet called Frederick Douglass "liberty's voice. . . ." He has been called the "black patriarch," the first of the great American black leaders. But how did he feel about himself?

Underneath all the titles, the honors, the applause, and later, even the jeers and sneers, there was a human being: a man, a husband and father, Frederick Douglass. He laughed and cried, got angry and learned to love, hoped and dreamed, lived and died. Let's see what he was really like.

Frederick was fortunate to have his Grandmama Betsey look after him when he was a young child.

Chapter 1

HARRIET, GRANDMAMA BETSEY, AND AUNT KATY

> Of my father I know nothing. Slavery had no recognition of fathers, as none of families. That the mother was a slave was enough for its deadly purpose. By its law the child followed the condition of its mother. The father might be a freeman and the child a slave. The father might be a white man, glorying in the purity of his Anglo-Saxon blood, and the child ranked with the blackest slaves. Father he might be, but not be husband, and could sell his own child without incurring reproach, if in its veins coursed one drop of African blood.

From *Life and Times of Frederick Douglass*
by Frederick Douglass

Sometime around February 1817, Harriet Bailey chose a grand name for her newborn son: Frederick Augustus Washington Bailey. The name didn't change the fact that the baby increased the slave holdings of Captain Aaron Anthony by one.

The mother knew she only had a short time to spend with her infant son. Master Anthony ordered all his slave women back to the fields within a week after delivery, their babies to be raised by others.

Betsey and Isaac Bailey were too old for field work, so Master Anthony made them responsible for all the slave babies born on the plantation. The children stayed with the Baileys until they were seven or eight years old. Then they were taken to the main plantation located in Talbot County on Maryland's Eastern Shore. There, another slave, also appointed by Master Anthony, supervised the children until they were able to care for themselves.

Harriet Bailey had no choice but to obey her master's orders. Bitter though it must have been, she surrendered her baby. There was one consolation. Harriet could take comfort in knowing that Frederick would be living with his natural grandparents. The elderly Baileys were Harriet's mother and father.

Frederick spent the first seven years of his life with Grandmama Betsey and Grandpapa Isaac. His early childhood years were filled with wonder, surprise, play, and learning.

Little Fred enjoyed living in his grandparents' two-story

cabin. To the young boy it was like a palace. Years later he described it as it was:

> Its fence-railed floor . . . upstairs, and its clay floor downstairs, its dirt and straw chimney, and windowless sides, and that most curious piece of workmanship, the ladder stairway . . .

The cabin was a quiet place located twelve or more miles away from the plantation's Great House. During this time in his life, the boy was not exposed to the harsh realities of slavery. Little Fred heard Grandmama Betsey say she "belonged" to a person called "Old Master," but as far as Fred was concerned he belonged to Grandmama. Even though he knew the word *master*, to a small boy the concept of being owned was much too difficult to understand, and too frightening to think about. The idea of not living with Grandmama Betsey was unthinkable.

She often told him "you are my boy." And that seemed to satisfy any concerns little Fred had at that time about slavery. He did have questions about his mother.

Sometimes late at night, a visitor came to see him. He learned she was his mother. She was one of Grandmama Betsey's five daughters who worked as a field hand on various farms at Tuckahoe owned by Captain Anthony. Harriet came as often as she could. After working all day in the fields, she walked for many miles to spend a few hours with her son. Then, she walked all night to be back in time for work the next morning.

Fred remembered waking from sleep and hearing his mother's gentle voice and feeling her smooth face next to his. He remembered thinking how beautiful she was. Fred loved his mother. He never forgot her, even though the night visits were few.

"Where does she go?" "Why can't I go with her?" The boy asked these and many more questions. The answers were always the same: "You'll find out in time."

But, meanwhile, young Fred enjoyed living under the protective and loving wing of his grandmother. She filled his daily life with joy and happiness. Perhaps she felt this love would have to last him a lifetime.

It was not uncommon to see Grandmama Betsey and little Fred picking blackberries or gathering kindling for a fire. Only Grandmama Betsey knew how to keep sweet potato plants alive through the winter. She sold the seedlings in the spring in exchange for a share of the buyer's crop in the fall. Some farmers even wanted her to plant the small seedlings, saying that she was blessed with a special touch. Anything she planted was sure to grow. Grandmama Betsey was a skilled and well-respected midwife, too. And, no doubt Fred was influenced by his grandfather, who, he learned later, was a free man.

So, although Frederick Augustus Washington Bailey was a slave child, snatched away from his mother at birth, he spent his formative years in a loving, caring environment free from the horrors of slavery. This early time passed swiftly.

One summer morning, Grandmama Betsey took Fred by the hand. Like any inquisitive child, he wanted to know where they were going. His grandmother didn't answer. Since it was not unusual for him to tag along with her on chores, Fred wasn't too concerned; he followed willingly. Soon his legs grew tired. His bare feet hurt. He wondered where they were going. They'd never gone that far from the cabin before.

Once again, Fred questioned his grandmother about where they were going. Grandmama Betsey groaned softly. The truth lay heavy on her heart. She didn't answer. Instead, the grandmother picked up her grandson and carried him.

The look on her face troubled the boy. What could cause Grandmama to look so sad, he wondered? Feeling that he was in some way the cause, he asked to be put down. "I can walk by myself," he said bravely. "Where are we going?" he asked again. Still, there was no answer.

Fear came. Little Fred imagined all kinds of horrible

things lurking in the dark woods. But, nothing imaginary was as horrible as the reality he had yet to face. For protection the child clutched the tail of his grandmother's skirt and plodded along wondering, wondering.

By late afternoon, Fred and Grandmama Betsey reached the Great House. It was large and beautiful and the boy was impressed, though still frightened. After a while he began to relax; he even ventured outside the kitchen door to play with a few children. He learned that the children were his brother, Perry, and his sisters Eliza and Sarah. He never knew he had a brother and sisters. He was excited, and about to ask Grandmama Betsey more about them, when a child came running from the kitchen. "Fed, Fed," the boy cried. "Grandmamma gone!"

Panic seized Fred. He rushed into the kitchen. He searched for his grandmother everywhere. Surely she was hiding, playing a joke, perhaps. That had to be it. Then, slowly he realized what had happened. Grandmama Betsey had left him. She was gone. He fell upon the ground and wouldn't be consoled. He cried himself sick.

"My brother gave me peaches . . ." Frederick wrote many years later, "but I promptly threw them on the ground." He had never felt so hurt or alone in his young life.

That afternoon Frederick Augustus Washington Bailey had reached the end of his childhood. That day was the beginning of his life as a slave. It was, however, a life he stubbornly refused to accept from that first day his grandmother left him at the Great House to his death. He would never see his grandmother again.

Seven-year-old Frederick Bailey was introduced to his new guardian, Aunt Katy. Captain Anthony had placed her in charge of all the slave children who lived on the main plantation.

Aunt Katy was an ornery woman as different from Grandmama Betsey as vinegar is to syrup. Aunt Katy formed a special dislike for her new charge. Crying angered her. "Hush," she yelled, "or I'll give you something to cry about." And she did.

Time and time again, Fred found himself the victim of Aunt Katy's quick temper and heavy hand. She took an almost demonic delight in brutalizing him with a stick or lashing out at him with a hard kick. One of Aunt Katy's favorite punishments was starvation. She wouldn't feed Fred for a full day if he did anything to displease her. And he always seemed to displease her in one way or another.

The boy grew mean and hostile. The harder he was beaten, the more determined he was not to behave. He deliberately did things to vex Aunt Katy and openly disobeyed her. But his behavior only brought Aunt Katy's wrath down on his back.

17

One day, when Fred had angered Aunt Katy greatly, he was sentenced to no food for the whole day. By evening, the boy was so hungry he stole a few kernels of corn. Aunt Katy caught him and was about to skin his hide, when his mother burst through the door.

Her black skin was glossy with perspiration and her eyes were set with anger. Aunt Katy knew better than to confront an angry mother defending her child. She backed down for the time being. She'd get the boy later.

Harriet had brought her son food wrapped in a handkerchief. She sat quietly while he ate. His introduction to slavery had been a cruel one. The boy hugged his mother and begged her to take him with her. Even as he pleaded, he knew that what he asked was impossible.

Harriet stayed with Fred until he cried himself to sleep. When he woke, like all the other times, his mother was gone. This time, Fred would never see his mother again. Harriet Bailey died not long afterward. From that time on, he had to fend for himself.

Chapter 2

LUCRETIA AND SOPHIA AULD

> I have since learned that she [my mother] was
> the only one of all the colored people of Tucka-
> hoe who could read. . . . In view of this fact, I am
> happy to attribute any love of letters I may
> have, not to my presumed Anglo-Saxon pater-
> nity, but to the native genius of my . . . mother—
> a woman who belonged to a race whose mental
> endowments are still disparaged and despised.

From *Life and Times of Frederick Douglass*
by Frederick Douglass

Grandmama Betsey had taken Frederick to the Great
House that was located on the Lloyd estate. Colonel Edward
Lloyd was the richest man in Talbot County, Maryland. Captain Aaron Anthony served as the general manager of the
Lloyd estates. While in Lloyd's service, Anthony acquired a
small personal fortune, and bought land and had overseers
as well as slaves of his own.

The Lloyd plantation was divided into several small farms. At each farm, overseers were in charge of day-to-day operations. It was common practice in that area for slaves to be hired out to do field work for small, independent farmers as well. The slaves worked; the masters collected their wages. Frederick's mother had been hired out to one of those farms.

Both Lloyd and Anthony lived at the main plantation, which was situated on the Eastern Shore of Maryland. Aunt Katy was owned by Lloyd, and served as his cook. She took care of Anthony's slave children also.

Although he disliked his new home, Frederick found some pleasure in exploring his new environment. On the plantation there were two extremes: wealth and poverty.

Colonel Lloyd's plantation was typical of the large southern estates of that time. On the grounds was a windmill, the overseer's house, and the "long quarters," where the house servants lived. Nearer the fields was a cluster of makeshift huts called the "quarters." Here the field slaves lived in crowded and filthy conditions.

Captain Anthony's house was long and low, nestled comfortably between two shade trees. Beyond his house sat an assortment of other buildings: barns, a horse stable, tobacco sheds, smokehouses, and a chicken coop.

The Great House was the largest and grandest structure

in the county. It was a stately mansion built in the Georgian architectural style that was popular in the nineteenth century. The two-story, white frame building was surrounded by poplar trees, lush green lawns, and magnificent flower gardens adorned with fountains and pools. Across the front of the house was a large balcony supported by two large columns. Behind the house were woods abundant with all kinds of wildlife.

Food was given out once a month to the slaves. Once a year, Anthony issued clothing and other supplies such as blankets and cooking utensils. The children were allotted a shirt, which hung like a dress on both boys and girls. Children weren't given shoes, jackets, trousers, or underwear. When the shirt tore, the child went ragged. When the shirt wore out, the child went naked, unless someone took pity and made him another one. Aunt Katy never did any mending or patching.

"In the day time," Frederick wrote in his autobiography, "I could protect myself by keeping on the sunny side of the house, or, in stormy weather, in the corner of the kitchen chimney. But the great difficulty was to keep warm during the night." Because he had no bed or blanket, young Frederick slept inside a feed bag.

Twice a day Aunt Katy prepared a coarse cornmeal mush and dumped it into a long trough. It was placed on the floor or outside on the ground. The children knelt before the slop and ate with shells or pieces of tree bark. While Old Master ate at a table richly decorated and bountifully laden, his slave children (for he had fathered some of them) were fed like hogs.

Reflecting on his childhood many years later, Frederick wrote that if he pushed or shoved to get in, Aunt Katy pulled him out and wouldn't let him eat until all the others had finished. If he resisted, he was beaten. Oppression bred cruelty. "Everybody in the South seemed to want the privilege of whipping somebody else," Frederick added.

Fred was a beautiful child with sad, brown eyes. Captain Anthony called him *his* "little Indian boy." And young Fred also caught the eye of Captain Anthony's daughter, Lucretia Auld.

Miss Lucretia, as she was called, has been described as a decent human being, whose kindness was considered weakness in a slaveholder. She saw a mistreated child, and reached out to him as far as she dared. So began an odd friendship. Miss Lucretia would send Frederick to do a chore. His payment would be a piece of buttered bread. The next day it was the same, except his treat would be a piece of fruit.

The two played a game. Frederick would stand outside Miss Lucretia's window and sing. She would appear at the window. "What little bird is that I hear singing?" she'd ask. Then she would send Fred to do a simple chore in exchange for food. In this way, Frederick was kept from starving. He came daily to get handouts from his mistress.

One day, Miss Lucretia told Frederick, "I have a wonderful surprise. You're going to live in Baltimore." Frederick was delighted. Anything—anywhere—had to be better than living with Aunt Katy. Two weeks later, eight-year-old Frederick boarded the boat that would take him to his new home. He had bathed in the creek. And Miss Lucretia had given him a new set of traveling clothes.

All the way he wondered what Baltimore was going to be like. Baltimore? The city had been incorporated in 1797. By 1825, when Frederick arrived there, it had become the largest city in Maryland. Baltimore was a bustling seaport where the shipbuilding industry was developing rapidly. Trade was steady and vigorous.

Frederick instantly loved his new home. Watching the sailors coming and going, listening to the constant chatter of people dickering over prices in the marketplace: all was very different from the rural farm rhythms of the Eastern Shore.

In Baltimore, Frederick felt freer. But he was quickly reminded that he was a slave, *owned* by Captain Aaron Anthony. He had been allowed to live with the Aulds on loan.

His job was to be personal companion to Tommy Auld, Miss Lucretia's nephew.

Frederick didn't think it was possible, but Miss Sophia Auld, his new mistress, was kinder than Miss Lucretia. She, too, has been described as a very kind and decent person.

Sophia Auld was a very religious woman who practiced her beliefs devoutly. Her husband, Hugh Auld, was neither kind nor pious. Since Frederick's only responsibility was to keep his son Tommy happy (a job Frederick didn't mind doing), Hugh Auld left the care of both boys to his wife.

For the first two years, life couldn't have been better for Frederick. Miss Sophia wasn't a slave owner so she didn't know the taboos involved in a master-slave relationship. She treated Frederick like one human should treat another.

"Look at me when you talk," she insisted, not knowing that slaves were expected to address all white people with downcast eyes. Frederick thought it strange for his mistress to insist that he stand erect and speak to her directly. But he also knew it was not his place to correct the mistress in any way. The boy simply did as he was told—and enjoyed it.

Frederick was well fed and slept on clean linen; he had shoes and clothing. Miss Sophia taught him table manners and how to speak politely.

Hugh Auld was preoccupied with his business and didn't, or chose not to, notice what was going on in his household.

He seemed unaware that his wife was treating a slave child with the same love and affection she gave her own son. For the first time since Grandmama Betsey's house, Frederick felt like he really belonged to someone—to a family.

Then quite unexpectedly Captain Anthony died. Old Master was dead. Frederick thought he should feel sorry, but he wasn't, and he didn't like pretending. But he became worried when word came that he had to return to Tuckahoe. He was part of Aaron Anthony's estate and all property (slaves included) had to be divided between Anthony's two children. Fortunately, Frederick was given to Miss Lucretia who immediately returned him to Baltimore. The fate of Grandmama Betsey was different. She was awarded to Andrew Anthony, a man described as "without compassion."

The boy's return to Baltimore was as tearful as his departure. He was never happier to be "home," for he had come to love Miss Sophia and little Tommy as family.

Life at the Aulds took up where it had been temporarily interrupted. Sophia Auld read to the boys regularly, Tommy tucked under one arm, and Frederick leaning on her lap. As Tommy learned his ABCs, so did Frederick. As Tommy learned to count from one to ten, so did Frederick.

Sophia Auld was proud of her teaching accomplishments. She did not know it was illegal to teach a slave to read. One evening she had the boys read before her husband. Much to her surprise, Hugh Auld was not pleased. He was furious.

"Do you know what you've done? Do you want to be thrown in jail?" he shouted angrily.

Miss Sophia was obviously shaken by her husband's outburst. Not wanting to displease him any more than she had, Miss Sophia quickly promised to stop teaching Frederick at once.

Hugh Auld gave his wife a crash course in how to keep a slave in his proper place. Although what she was required to do was against her beliefs, she acquiesced without complaint.

At first, Miss Sophia's opposition to his reading hurt and confused Frederick. He wrote later: "Nature made us friends, but slavery had made us enemies. . . . She had changed, and . . . I too, had changed. We were both victims to the same overshadowing evil, she as mistress, I as slave."

Frederick overheard Master Hugh say, "If you give a nigger an inch he will take an ell [mile]. . . . If he learns to read . . . he'll be running away with himself."

Although the Aulds had forbidden Frederick to read again, he disobeyed their orders and read whatever and whenever he could. However, to stay in good favor with the Aulds, Frederick respected the other restrictions placed on him. But he was more determined than ever to read and learn.

Whenever possible, Frederick tried to increase his vocabulary and to understand the meanings of words. In words he felt there was the magic of ideas. For example, one evening Frederick heard master Auld arguing with one of his guests about the "abolitionists." Frederick had never heard the word and wanted to know what it meant.

Later he found newspapers in the trash can and sneaked them into his room. He learned that "abolitionists" were people who wanted to get rid of slavery in the United States. Some abolitionists were white people! White people against slavery? Frederick was pleasantly surprised. It made him feel good knowing that there were white men and women who spoke *openly* against slavery. He never would have known that had he not been able to read. Yes, reading was magical—and dangerous to those who wanted to keep him enslaved. Frederick decided to learn as much as he could.

Growing up in Baltimore, Frederick made many friends. Some of them were white youths who accepted him as a companion and not as a slave. In his autobiography, he wrote: "I do not remember ever while I was in slavery, to have met a *boy* who defended the system, but I do remember many times, when I was consoled by them, and . . . encouraged to hope that something would yet occur by which I would be made free."

His friends bought him books and newspapers. From them Frederick learned more about abolition. He read that some Baltimoreans wanted slavery ended. Yet, there were those who justified slavery by saying God intended it. The city was full of angry discussions. Frederick quietly read the newspapers and wondered what it all meant.

The years passed quickly and Frederick became a teenager. The Aulds allowed him to come and go without too many questions. He used his free time to study. He began to question his actions. Was his disobedience to the Aulds wrong? Was it really the way he'd been taught? Did God create some men to be masters and some to be slaves? By rejecting slavery, was he going against God's will?

At age thirteen, Frederick read *The Columbian Orator*, a schoolbook. It helped him find answers. In the book were speeches delivered by leaders who spoke against human oppression and injustices. He read the writings of Richard Brinsley Sheridan, an English dramatist and politician, who boldly denounced oppression and spoke forcefully for human rights. He read William Pitt and George Fox. There he learned that those who would keep a people enslaved, first convince them that it is God's will for them to be slaves. Resistance would then mean going against God. Frederick recognized that argument very well. It was the slave owners' major defense. And it convinced many. But, after reading Pitt and Fox, and others, Frederick rejected slavery without guilt of any kind. He wrote: "God had nothing to do with slavery. It is blasphemy to even suggest that He does!"

With that issue clear in his mind, young Frederick "confessed religion" under the guidance of Pastor Charles Lawson, a free black man. Pastor Lawson became a father figure to Frederick. His influence helped fill a void in the boy's life left by Miss Sophia.

She and Frederick hardly spoke except to exchange an order and acknowledgment. Her son Tommy was no longer little. He was a school-age boy, learning how to read, write, and become a proper master. To him, Frederick was a servant and addressed in a master-servant manner. They were no longer friends.

Then came the Southampton Insurrection of 1831, led by Nat Turner. Slave owners were horrified by him; slaves were inspired by him.

Nat Turner had been a slave in Southampton County, Virginia. Turner learned to hate slavery from his mother, a native African. His master's son taught him to read. Turner fervently embraced religion and thought God expected him to lead his people out of slavery. The South was darkened by a solar eclipse in February 1831. Turner decided it was a sign that God wanted him to lead an uprising among the slaves.

On the night of August 21, 1831, with seven others, Nat Turner slaughtered his master and his master's family.

Then, he moved to the next plantation. The uprising was short-lived; Turner's army never numbered more than seventy-five. Around fifty white people were killed. The state militia crushed the rebellion and many innocent slaves were killed along with some of Turner's followers.

In the end, Nat Turner was captured and hanged. Twelve slaves were sent into the Deep South. There they were worked until they dropped dead from exhaustion, starvation, disease, or all three.

Nat Turner's insurrection frightened slave owners. They never believed slaves would revolt. As a result restrictions were tightened against education, movement, and assembly of slaves. To many, Turner's actions marked the beginning of a long and bitterly-fought war to end slavery.

Frederick knew of Turner's revolt. He, too, wanted freedom. Freedom was *always* on Frederick's mind. Although he thought about running away and had the opportunity to do so, he didn't believe that the time was right. Within three months he would wish he'd run as far and fast as he could.

Chapter 3

THOMAS AULD AND EDWARD COVEY

It was now more than seven years since I had lived with Master Thomas Auld, in the family of my old master, Capt. Anthony, on the home plantation of Col. Lloyd. I knew him then as the husband of old master's daughter. I had now to know him as my master. . . .

There was, in the Bay-side, very near the campground . . . a man named Edward Covey, who enjoyed the reputation of being a first rate hand at breaking young Negroes.

From *Life and Times of Frederick Douglass* by Frederick Douglass

Frederick was sixteen years old in 1833, the same year slavery was abolished throughout the British Empire. The irony, of course, was that Frederick might have been freed in America, too, if the colonists had lost the Revolutionary War. Black men, however, were some of the strongest supporters of the Revolutionary cause—men like Crispus Attucks who died in the Boston Massacre, March 5, 1770, and Peter Salem and Prince Whipple who, in 1775, fought with General George Washington at Bunker Hill. Yet, for all their gallantry, many black revolutionary soldiers found themselves re-enslaved after the war ended, and by 1792, the United States Congress had restricted service in the army to white men only. The exception was Andrew Jackson who, in the War of 1812, granted freedom to the slaves who fought with him.

Unfortunately for Frederick and other slaves, the road to freedom was a much longer and more winding one. Despite the black man's contribution to the birth of a free nation, slavery flourished in the United States, especially after the invention of the cotton gin by Eli Whitney in 1793. Money and slavery made a powerful bond. "King Cotton" became the master. Cotton markets would seal the fate of the slave, the slaveholder, and the nation. But, Frederick later wrote: "Nature has done almost nothing to prepare men and women to be either slave or slaveholders."

In 1833, Frederick was ordered to return to Maryland's Eastern Shore where he would spend five unforgettable years. During that time he would be tested to the limits of his physical, mental, and emotional endurance.

Frederick had a new master. Lucretia Auld died and her

husband, Thomas Auld, became the owner of all her holdings, including Frederick. Thomas and Hugh Auld had a brotherly disagreement and, in anger, Thomas ordered Frederick back to the Eastern Shore. At that time Thomas Auld was operating a store near St. Michaels and he hired out Frederick to farmers in the area.

It was difficult for Frederick to leave his friends, especially the fatherly Pastor Lawson. Baltimore had been his home for eight years. Going back was more difficult than he ever imagined.

Thomas Auld married quickly after Miss Lucretia's death. His second wife, Rowena Auld, was as cruel as she was greedy. She encouraged Thomas, who didn't need much persuasion, to increase slave work loads and decrease their food rations. The Aulds worked their slaves to near exhaustion and starvation.

Frederick knew hard work and hunger for the first time since he was seven years old. Hunger led him to steal. If he found the smokehouse open, he stole enough food for himself and others. He earned a reputation for being quite a rogue. But he never thought of himself as a thief.

He reasoned: "At first he [Auld] owned it [the food] in the tub, and last he owned it in me."

During the summer of 1833, Thomas Auld was baptized and joined a church. Frederick questioned his master's motives, but gave him the benefit of the doubt. Perhaps Auld had been converted. Although Frederick didn't expect Auld to free all his slaves, he did expect him to begin treating them humanely.

Nothing changed. Being a church member put Thomas Auld in good standing with his neighbors, but toward his slaves he remained steadfastly cruel. Frederick wondered how such men could be respected in the community of mankind. It helped him to know that there were people— abolitionists—who denounced those who claimed brotherly love on one hand, and kept men in chains with the other hand.

Years later Frederick said in a speech: "Absolute and arbitrary power can never be maintained by one man over the body and soul of another man, without brutal chastisement and enormous cruelty."

The young man's attitude became increasingly more hostile; his actions more openly defiant. He earned the title of "bad nigger."

At the same time Frederick was questioning Auld's religious motives, he was also questioning some of his own. Pastor Lawson had taught Frederick to use the biblical "turn the other cheek" doctrine toward his master. How many times, the boy asked himself, am I expected to take the blows that trample my person into the dust? How long am I expected to endure the kicks that cripple my spirit? He had no friend like Pastor Lawson in whom he could confide. Young Frederick had seen the result of slaves who had been pushed to their limits. Once, when he was a boy, he had seen Rigby Hopkins beat a slave severely. When the slave had taken more lashes than believed humanly possible, something inside the man had clicked. His body stiffened, ramrod straight. The slave stood before his master, Hopkins, and said, "You can shoot me, but you can't whip me." Miraculously, he was not shot or whipped any more. His resistance was said to have been caused by insanity, and from then on, he was called a "crazy nigger." In the eyes of the master, that slave was no longer useful, so he was turned out, sent into the woods to die alone, an outcast. Other slaves were forbidden to have anything to do with him.

Frederick knew that the sword of resistance had a double edge. The overseer held the power of judge, jury, and executioner. A seasoned overseer, one who had a reputation to defend as well as the status quo of slavery to maintain, often responded differently, as did one of Captain Anthony's overseers, Austin Gore.

Frederick had been told as a boy that a fellow slave named Bill Denby had refused to take a beating. Without pause Gore had shot Denby in the head. But, to the master, a dead slave was wasted money.

Frederick knew that the time was rapidly coming when he wouldn't be able to turn the other cheek any longer. What was going to happen when he didn't?

When word spread that Frederick could read, the slaves asked him to start a Sunday school for black children, which he promptly did. On some plantations slaves were permitted to hold church services as long as the teachings were biblical in content. Frederick's reading of the Bible was tolerated, if not appreciated by his master.

Frederick held a few Sunday school sessions, but one Sunday morning, services were interrupted by a mob of white men who came with sticks and clubs and drove them off. Thomas Auld, Frederick's master, was among them. Frederick offered no resistance; it would be useless, he thought. The Sunday school was ended. And, within the week, Thomas Auld sent Frederick to a slave breaker named Edward Covey.

A slave breaker was a man who earned a living by turning uncontrollable slaves into satisfied servants. And, Covey was considered the best slave breaker in all Maryland, praised by owners for his work, and feared by all those who might come under his authority.

On January 1, 1834, Frederick was delivered to Covey's farm for the period of one year. Frederick had never done field work. Yet he and two other men, Bill Smith and Bill

Hughes, were expected to work over four hundred acres alone. Edward Covey rode on horseback taunting them, pushing them to work harder. Day after day, from sunrise to sunset, no matter what the weather, they worked in the fields. It was a miserable existence.

Covey was particularly hard on Frederick. Every opportunity he could find, Covey beat the boy or denied him food. If the boy stopped working long enough to wipe the sweat from his brow, Covey accused him of being lazy and gave him extra chores or beat him. If the youngster didn't move to his liking, Covey beat him; if the boy didn't speak quickly enough, or spoke too soon, Covey beat him. Frederick was beaten so often his back was one mass of open flesh. For months he was starved and worked nearly to death.

Covey gave everybody a day of rest on Sunday. Frederick usually collapsed under a tree and tended his wounds, ate the slop that was given to him, and then slept fitfully. Of that time he wrote later: "The disposition to read departed; the cheerful spark that lingered about my eye died; the dark night of slavery closed in upon me; and behold a man transformed into a brute!"

Frederick forgot how to feel, how to care. He thought of suicide, but he was too afraid—not of dying, but of Covey. Covey had convinced the boy that he couldn't commit suicide without permission.

In August, a year after Thomas Auld became a Christian, Frederick ran away from Covey's farm and told his master "all the circumstances, as well as I [Frederick] could . . ." Frederick presented his case in a reasonably subdued manner. Auld looked for signs that might show his rebellious slave had been properly trained. Frederick spoke so pleadingly, Auld was almost persuaded. The point was not to kill the slave, but to make him more manageable. From all outward appearances, Frederick seemed changed. But Thomas offered one more test.

"You're not hurt. You're not dizzy," said Master Thomas.

Frederick wisely didn't argue. Auld was, no doubt, taking note of how he responded. "What do you want me to do?" Auld then asked.

"Please assign me to another. I am sure Mr. Covey will kill me if I return," Frederick said, being careful to add "sir" at the end.

But he was not careful enough. Frederick had made the mistake Auld was looking for. Auld pretended to be furious. "You still haven't learned," he shouted in an angry voice. Auld ranted and raved about how Frederick had openly accused a God-fearing white man of being capable of murder. "You're still arrogant," shouted Auld. "Besides, if you leave Covey now," Frederick heard his master say, "I should lose your wages for the entire year. . . . You *must go back*."

Frederick knew that his master was not concerned about the pain and suffering he had endured, but about the money he could earn.

After seeing Frederick's festering wounds, Auld agreed to let him stay the night. But, the boy was ordered back to Covey at "first light."

Frederick remembered that night well: "I remained . . . all night . . . and in the morning (Saturday) I started off, obedient to the order of Master Thomas, feeling that I had no friend on earth, and doubting if I had one in heaven."

The slave boy reached the slave breaker's farm at about nine in the morning. Covey, "the Snake," as he was called, lay waiting for him. He surprised Frederick and would have caught him, but the boy was motivated by pure fear. He escaped. Frederick knew Covey was capable of killing him, so he ran into the woods. There he hid until nightfall. Too afraid to stay there, and too afraid to go back, he slumped near a tree and wept. Soon, he fell asleep.

During the night, Frederick was awakened by footsteps. He hugged a nearby tree, hoping to be unnoticed. To his surprise a black man stood before him.

Sandy Jenkins, a slave, was married to a free woman. He was permitted to visit his wife on Sundays. That's where Sandy was going when he found Frederick. He took the boy to his cabin. Sandy's wife, said to be an Indian woman, prepared them a hot meal and dressed the boy's wounds. Frederick felt better, but he still had a problem—Covey!

While they were thinking about what to do, Sandy blurted out that he understood the magic of roots and herbs. "Some," he said, "have powers that can keep you safe." Sandy said he remembered these things from his homeland in Africa. He said such an herb grew in the woods and he would find its root.

Frederick wrote later that Sandy told him if he wore the root "it would be impossible for Covey to strike me . . ."

Frederick would have laughed had the situation not been so grave. He accepted the root, but didn't believe it had any power. "How," he thought later, "did I know but that the hand of the Lord was in it?"

Frederick went back to Covey's place with the intention of falling on his face and begging for his life. But it was early Sunday morning, and Covey was on his way to church. Covey greeted him so pleasantly that Frederick wondered if in some way Covey had been miraculously altered. But then came Monday morning.

Covey called Frederick to the barn to take care of the horses. Frederick believed Covey was going to beat him to death, and Master Auld wouldn't care. There was barely one thread of hope left in him. Nobody cared! All hope was gone. The thread snapped.

Once he accepted his death, fear left. And he made a decision borne out of that hopelessness. He entered the barn, determined to die on his feet and not cowering in a corner like an animal. You can kill me, he said to himself, but I won't be beaten anymore.

Covey sneaked into the barn and grabbed Frederick by the leg and brought him down. Frederick didn't strike Covey, but he resisted Covey's attempts to hold him down and tie him.

Stunned by his actions, Covey called for help. Now there were two against one. Frederick kicked out and sent Covey's assistant howling in pain. The odds were even again. Covey got the best of Frederick and held him in a bear hug. But the boy would not fall or submit.

One of the workers came from visiting his wife. "Take hold of him," Covey yelled. The man pretended he didn't hear and moved on. Covey shouted for someone to help him, but in the end he was forced to handle Frederick alone. Even in his weakened condition, the boy was stronger than Covey, and they both knew it.

Covey held the slave for two exhausting hours, neither willing to give in. At last, Covey hurled Frederick to the ground. "Now, you scoundrel," he yelled fiercely, "go to your work; I would not have whipped you half so hard if you had not resisted."

Years later, Frederick wrote in his autobiography: "The fact was, he had not whipped me at all. . . . During the whole six months that I lived with Covey after this transaction, he never again laid the weight of his finger on me in anger."

Frederick remembered the old saying from his childhood: "He who is whipped easiest is whipped most often." From that day on he believed it to be a true statement.

On December 25, 1835, Frederick left Covey's service. He was happy to leave, although, by that time, Covey was quite "broken."

Chapter 4

WILLIAM FREELAND

For my part, I had become altogether too big
for my chains.

From *Life and Times of Frederick Douglass*
by Frederick Douglass

In January 1835, Frederick was hired out by Thomas
Auld to Mr. William Freeland. Freeland thought himself a
gentleman and wouldn't dream of "indulging in the cruel
occupation of overseer." His only concern was that the fields
were worked. How and by whom didn't seem to matter.

Frederick was happy to learn that Sandy Jenkins, the
slave who had given him the protective root, was at Freeland's place. Frederick told Sandy what had happened with
Covey. Sandy was convinced the root had provided the protection. Frederick didn't argue the point, but he had reasoned it out another way.

Frederick's resistance had put Covey in a difficult situation. If Covey had killed Frederick, Auld would have forced

the slave breaker to pay the full price of a slave. Or, Covey could have pressed charges against Frederick. In that case Frederick would have been branded or hanged. Pressing charges would have exposed Covey. He would have admitted publicly that a seventeen-year-old had gotten the better of him. Covey depended upon his reputation as a slave breaker. Taking all matters into consideration, Frederick believed Covey shrewdly chose to let what happened pass unnoticed.

Frederick wisely decided not to say anything about the matter either. He feared what Master Auld might do. Once a slave was considered too bad to handle, he was usually sold into the Deep South. To Maryland slaves that was an automatic death sentence. Covey didn't want to be exposed. Frederick didn't want to be sold. So, the two reached an unspoken agreement: "I won't say anything if you won't."

At Freeland's farm, the situation was at least tolerable. Frederick met Charles Roberts and Henry Bailey, a relative. He also formed a bonding friendship between two brothers named Henry and John Harris. They became the family Frederick always wanted.

As his body and mind healed, Frederick's dreams of freedom returned. They were strong, compelling dreams. They made him restless. He shared his thoughts and dreams with his new family of friends.

So determined was he to run away, he promised himself that he would be a free man before the new year dawned again. He was so sure about it, others around him began to believe that they, too, might be free. Plans were made to escape.

Freeland allowed his slave workers to have Sunday school, insisting that they study only scripture. Frederick and his friends used the opportunity to discuss their escape. Frederick often used Bible stories as a way of talking about freedom. The slaves knew Bible stories well. The same stories were part of their oral tradition, told using different characters in a different setting, perhaps, but somehow very much the same.

The Moses story was a slave favorite, as was David and Goliath's story, or any tale about the small, weak, and oppressed overcoming the seemingly strong. More and more, Frederick was becoming the leader of a small group who shared his desire to be free.

Frederick wrote in his autobiography: "These meetings must have resembled, on a small scale, the meetings of the revolutionary conspirators in their primary condition. We were plotting against our (so-called) lawful rulers, with this difference—we sought our own good, and not the harm of our enemies. We did not seek to overthrow them, but to escape from them."

Henry, John, and the others knew that if they were caught planning an escape, they could be sold into the Deep South. But, even at age eighteen, Frederick spoke convincingly. He talked about freedom, using impressive language that gave them courage to face the unknown. The cost of freedom was high. But they all seemed willing to pay whatever price was necessary.

For weeks the group detailed their plans. Although they were only a few hundred miles from a free state, they had no understanding of freedom in geographical terms. To them, freedom was a long way off. Getting there was as much a mental journey as it was a physical one. Frederick understood. He was patient with his friends. Slowly, he planned, step by step. He didn't want anyone to panic.

One day, Sandy told Frederick about a dream he had been having. To him it was a bad omen. Sandy's dream was this: He was awakened by angry birds. Frederick was in the claws of one of these big birds. He said the bird holding Frederick was surrounded by other large birds that seemed angry. While the large bird held Frederick, the smaller birds pecked at his eyes. Finally, the large bird holding Frederick tight in his grip flew away in a southeasterly direction. Sandy warned his friend to give up the escape plans. Frederick refused. Sandy asked to be counted out of the plans. He agreed, however, not to alarm the others.

46

The Harris brothers, Charles Roberts, Henry Bailey, and Frederick targeted the Easter holidays as the escape date.

The success of the plan rested on William Freeland. It was the custom of some slave masters to relax a few restrictions on holidays. All work ceased. Some children were allowed to visit their parents. Some husbands were allowed to visit their wives. Holidays were a welcome relief to the slave. On holidays a drinking man could get plenty of whiskey, and a praying man could meet, sing, and pray for as long as he chose. To the master's thinking, a drunken slave found his freedom in the bottom of the bottle, and a praying slave found his freedom in the stars. Neither slave would cause the master a problem, so he could relax a little himself.

Frederick was counting on this custom. He forged written passes for all the would-be runaways. With them, they could travel freely about without being suspected. Movement of slaves over a holiday was not uncommon. They would be long gone by the time they were missed.

Generally, Freeland trusted Frederick and the others. Freeland was a bit more relaxed than most masters. Frederick observed how easy it was to lull him into believing they were contented.

Frederick wrote later: "The remark in the olden time was . . . that slaves were the most contented and happy laborers in the world, and their dancing and singing were referred to in proof of this alleged fact; but it was a great mistake to suppose them happy . . ."

When the slaves sang and danced they were often sending coded messages to one another. The spirituals were sometimes used to communicate information about an escape attempt, to poke fun at the master, to predict the final downfall of slavery, or to say to one another "I know how you feel." Then other times, the spirituals were genuine forms of musical worship.

For example, the spiritual "Steal Away" began: ". . . steal away . . . steal away . . . steal away to Jesus . . ." This song told the slaves that somebody was going to run away.

Then, when word came back that the slave had gotten away, the success was transmitted by another song: "When I get to heaven, gon' put on my shoes and gon' walk all over God's heaven . . ." Slaves used this song to collectively rejoice for the one who had managed to make it to "heaven." Heaven was freedom to a slave. Every man, woman, and child slave knew that if they followed the North Star they'd eventually come to that wondrous place—freedom!

Often slave masters trained a slave from infancy to become a spy for him. Perhaps it was such a trained spy who betrayed Frederick and his friends. Or, perhaps, Freeland wasn't as off-guard as they thought. Regardless, the runaway plot was discovered.

The men never got to use their forged passes. The constable came to the Freeland farm. One by one the would-be runaways were questioned. Each man denied knowing anything.

Frederick described what happened years later. Mr. Freeland confronted the Harris brothers and Frederick in the kitchen. Frederick's hands were tied. When it came time for the constable to tie Henry's hands, he refused. Guns were drawn, but Henry shouted "*Shoot me*. You can't kill me but once. *Shoot, shoot!*" With that, Henry raised his arms and knocked their guns to the ground. His assailants pounced on him and beat him unconscious. Meanwhile during the scuffle, Frederick was able to throw his forged pass into the fire.

It was then that Frederick remembered Sandy's dream. His situation was much like what had been described. "I was in the hands of moral vultures . . . amid the jeers of new birds of the same feather . . ."

John and Frederick were bound together. "Eat your pass," Frederick whispered to each one of his friends. They did. The passes were the only evidence against any of them, because they had not actually run away.

All five men were taken to the Easton jail, about fifteen miles southeast of St. Michaels. Again, Sandy's dream came to mind: "And the birds flew away in a southeasterly direction . . ."

Actually, the only wrong they had committed was to look guilty. Fortunately, the forged notes had been destroyed. Charles and Henry were put in one cell together. The Harris brothers and Frederick were put together in another. They were told that Georgia slave traders were coming to buy them. That was the usual punishment for runaways: being sent to Georgia or Alabama where, according to rumor, *nobody* ever escaped. Among east coast slaves it was said, "Satan holds the keys to the Deep South."

Each master let his slave stay in jail long enough to scare him into submission. The Harris brothers were released first. They were warned against getting involved with troublemakers like Frederick. They were taken away, and Frederick never saw either of them again.

Then Henry Bailey and Charles Roberts were released one at a time, under the threat that when next they got into trouble they'd be sold without consideration.

Only Frederick remained in jail. Thomas Auld knew he was there, but took his time coming. Other slaveholders in the area were furious with Frederick. They insisted Auld get rid of him or they would.

Frederick remembered the time well: "Master Thomas . . . came to the prison . . . for the purpose, as he said, of sending me to Alabama with a friend of his, who would emancipate me at the end of eight years." Frederick knew that his chances of living eight years in Alabama were slim. So, he decided to do what his friends had done. When Master Auld came to the jail, Frederick begged for forgiveness. He called himself stupid, and tried to act repentant and show remorse.

Auld seemed unimpressed with Frederick's emotional display. He must have recognized it for what it was—a poorly performed show. Frederick was not a good faker. But, for reasons known only to Thomas Auld, he didn't sell Frederick to his Alabama friend. Auld sent him back to Baltimore to live with his brother, Hugh Auld.

Frederick happily boarded a steamer for Baltimore. Arriving there, he found the city much the same. It was still a fast-moving, rapidly growing seaport. However, things had changed on the political scene. The slave issue was a political stew pot, threatening to boil over at any moment.

In the Hugh Auld household much had changed, too. Tommy Auld was no longer a schoolboy. He was neither kind nor unkind to Frederick. It was as though the two had never met. Sophia Auld hardly spoke to Frederick either, passing him without saying a word. The little boy who had leaned on her lap and listened to stories had become a shadow person with form but no substance.

Frederick's orders were to act in all ways as though Hugh Auld were his master for life. He had promised Master Thomas Auld that he would be respectful and obedient. Of

course he would have promised anything to get away from the Eastern Shore.

It was clear to all who knew him before that Frederick had changed also. He was no longer an eight-year-old, wide-eyed little boy. He was eighteen. Physically, he had reached his mature height, well over six feet tall. In spite of his past ill treatment, he had grown into a handsome young man, with thick, curly hair, honey brown skin, and brown eyes that flashed steely gray when he was angry. His body, though healed, was badly scarred. So were his emotions. Learning to trust again, to feel again, to allow himself to care again, would take a long time.

Chapter 5

MASTER HUGH

> The slaveholders . . . by encouraging the enmity
> of the poor laboring white man against blacks,
> succeeded in making the said white man almost
> as much a slave as the black slave himself. . . .
> Both were plundered, and by the same plun-
> derers. The slave was robbed by his master of
> all his earnings . . . and the white laboring man
> was robbed by the slave system of the just
> results of his labor, because he was flung into
> competition with a class of laborers who worked
> without wages.

From *Life and Times of Frederick Douglass*
by Frederick Douglass

Thomas Auld sent Frederick to Baltimore to learn a
trade, promising that if he behaved himself, he would be
freed at age twenty-five. "The promise had but one fault,"
Frederick remembered. "It seemed too good to be true."

Owning a skilled slave was financially rewarding for an urban slave master. A skilled laborer—black or white—could demand top dollar in Baltimore in the 1830s. And all slave wages went to the master. But teaching a slave a skill was potentially dangerous. Skilled work built self-pride. A man who had self-pride would not tolerate slavery very long.

Learning a trade became very important to Frederick. He tried to be as cooperative as possible because he knew he'd be able to earn a living and take care of himself when free if he were a skilled worker.

After Frederick's arrival in Baltimore, Hugh Auld found him a job. William Gardiner, a shipbuilder, hired him saying, "Do whatever the carpenters tell you to do."

All day long twenty-five men kept young Fred very busy. There wasn't time to learn a trade. His official title was "apprentice," but he was little more than an errand boy. "Go get me this," or "Bring me that" was all he heard. Frederick didn't complain, fearing he might be considered arrogant. And he didn't want to risk being sent back to the Eastern Shore or worse.

Still it was difficult to control his own anger, and endure the hostility of the white workers toward him and other blacks on the docks. In an earlier time, the shipyard workers had been amiable; many had openly spoken against slavery. But things had changed. Frederick found the white carpenters at Gardiner's shop to be angry men who scarcely spoke to him without adding a swear word, coupled with "nigger" or "darky." From his friends, many of whom were black skilled laborers, he learned the reason for the anger.

For many years Baltimore's shipbuilders had used black and white laborers. Skilled and unskilled workers had toiled side by side, each man earning wages according to his work. A slave's wages, however, were paid to the master. Then white laborers decided it was degrading to work alongside slaves. They threatened to strike unless the blacks were paid less. The slaves were blamed for keeping the wages low. But it was not the slaves who set the price of their labor so low. It was their masters and the slave system in general. That issue was not addressed.

In 1838, Baltimore was a political hotbed. The primary issue was slavery. Every day Frederick endured the harassment of his fellow apprentices. Tension mounted. The verbal insults became more stinging. For the most part, Frederick ignored the insults, but if physically abused, he didn't hesitate to fight back.

He was strong and in a fair fight, one-on-one, Frederick could easily win. One day, in front of a large crowd, four men attacked him and beat him nearly to death. Their only reason was "he deserved it." People watched the beating and cheered.

Battered and hurt, Frederick stumbled home. Hugh Auld saw him and was told what had happened. He was furious. Sophia Auld attended Frederick's wounds and silently wept for him. He later wrote in his autobiography: "No mother's hand could have been more tender than hers. She bound up my head and covered my wounded eye with a lean piece of fresh beef. It was almost compensation for all I suffered . . . Her affectionate heart was not yet dead, though much hardened by time and circumstances."

Hugh Auld took his slave to a lawyer and demanded that the four men be arrested. Master Hugh was in for a surprise. The lawyer informed Auld that unless white witnesses agreed to testify, there was no case. Even though Frederick could identify the men who had beaten him, his testimony was not enough to issue a warrant.

In his autobiography Frederick recalled the injustice angrily: "He could issue no warrant, on my word, against white persons, and if I had been killed in the presence of a *thousand blacks*, their testimony combined would have been insufficient to condemn a single murderer."

Hugh Auld wouldn't let his slave go back to Gardiner's shop. After his wounds healed, Frederick was hired out to another shipbuilder, Mr. Walter Pirce, who was also Hugh Auld's employer. There he learned to be a caulker, filling the seams of the ships with a waterproofing material. Within a year's time, Frederick was a very good caulker. He earned as much as seven dollars a week, which was top dollar for a journeyman caulker at that time. But, all his wages went to Master Hugh.

Every Saturday, Hugh Auld expected his slave to hand over his pay. That was the way the system worked, but it was forever a thorn in Frederick's side. To him it was unreasonable to ask a person to work, then expect that man to give all the wages of his labor to another man.

Perhaps Master Hugh felt guilty about taking all of Frederick's earnings. For whatever reason, he agreed to the following conditions which Frederick describes here: "I was to be allowed all my time; and make all bargains for work, and to collect my own wages; and in return . . . I was required . . . to pay him three dollars at the end of each week, and to board and clothe myself, and buy my own calking [sic] tools."

The arrangement worked well for master and slave. It gave Auld a more satisfied worker. It gave Frederick time to think, read, and plan. Thoughts of freedom occupied a great deal of his time on and off work.

One day at lunchtime, Frederick met Benny, a black sailor whose ship had sailed without him. It didn't seem to bother Benny; he'd made up his mind to stay in Baltimore. Frederick helped him get a job in the shipyard, and the two young men became friends. Frederick liked Benny's happy-go-lucky spirit, and Benny respected Frederick's serious nature.

Benny told Frederick he was going to a meeting of the East Baltimore Mental Improvement Society. He said that lots of pretty girls would be there.

Frederick hadn't thought too much about girls. He smiled and said he liked the name of the group. The idea of mental improvement was appealing. He agreed to go.

The group was composed of young free blacks who met on Sundays. They had lectures, musical selections, readings, and, in general, enjoyed themselves. Right away, Frederick felt self-conscious. He was the only slave there. All the others were free blacks. Benny introduced his guest when the chairman called on him to do so.

Slowly Frederick rose to accept the welcome. He was liked immediately, especially by the young ladies. After all, he was very handsome, and unmarried! He was welcomed back the following week, and the week after. He accepted graciously. It didn't matter to his new friends that he was a slave and they were free.

One of the young girls who didn't giggle all the time was Anna Murray. Frederick didn't want to admit it, but he liked her very much. He told Benny he was going to the meetings because he enjoyed the speeches and the good fellowship. But Benny teased him, saying that he thought Frederick was in love. Frederick denied it, stating that he had no time for love.

Soon Frederick's attitude changed. He'd begun to whistle, and his eyes twinkled. Benny teased him constantly. Finally there came a time when Frederick didn't deny it. Anna Murray was worth loving, but he worried that he might not be worthy of her love. The thought troubled him so much that he stopped talking to Anna and tried to avoid her. She was free. He was a slave. No free woman would want to be associated with a slave, he thought.

One evening Anna confronted Frederick. "Don't you think I could love you because you're a slave?" Frederick was silent. He felt his heart pounding. Then he found the courage he needed. He told Anna that one day he'd be free, and, when he was, he would want her to share his freedom. He asked Anna to be his wife. Anna promised Frederick that she would come to him wherever he was.

More than ever now, Frederick thought about running away. He had an even stronger reason to be free. Slaves who brought home their wages and didn't call attention to themselves could move freely about without difficulty. Frederick decided he always should comply with the wishes of Master Hugh and gain more free time, time he needed to plan his escape.

Then he almost made a mistake. One Saturday Frederick chose not to report his wages to Master Hugh. Instead, he went to the meeting as usual, thinking that he could give Auld his money the following morning. Frederick was mistaken. Master Hugh was furious and punished his slave by taking away all privileges. Frederick was not to do anything without permission!

As usual, Fred responded with his own brand of stubbornness. He wouldn't do one thing unless Master Hugh told him to do it. And that included work. He didn't go to work for a week, because Master Hugh hadn't told him what to do. When that Saturday came, there were no wages to report. Auld promised there would be more than enough work for him the following week.

It was then that Frederick told Benny the exact date of his planned escape: September 2, 1838—three weeks away.

Once his mind was made up, the plan moved swiftly. On his last Saturday with the Aulds, Frederick gave Master Hugh his regular payment of money. On Sunday he stayed away all day as was his custom. It raised no suspicion.

Monday, however, he was well on his way to freedom. Frederick sat nervously on the train. Dressed in Benny's sailor suit—a red shirt, black cravat tied in sailor fashion, and a tarpaulin hat—he didn't look the slightest bit out of place. But he felt like a criminal fleeing from justice. He had to keep reminding himself to stay calm. Nervousness would raise suspicion. Over and over he repeated the details of his escape in his mind.

In the state of Maryland, free blacks had to keep in their possession "free papers." He had borrowed Benny's "sailor's protection papers." His friend also had taken Frederick's baggage to the station. Just as the train had begun to pull away, Frederick had hopped on. The plan was to board the train without a ticket, for if he had gone into the station to purchase one, the ticket agent would have examined his papers. The borrowed papers described a man who in no way looked like Frederick.

Up to that point, all had gone as planned. Still Frederick was terrified. The conductor approached him and asked to see identification. When the conductor saw the familiar symbol on the seaman's protection papers, he sold Frederick a ticket and moved on without taking time to inspect the papers more closely. Frederick took a deep breath. The voyage was not over yet.

The train sped through Maryland, then crossed into Delaware. Delaware was a slave state. Twice, on board the train, Frederick saw people he knew. Either he was not recognized or they chose not to betray him. At Wilmington, Delaware, the runaway took a steamship up the Delaware River to Philadelphia. Again the borrowed papers were not closely inspected. In Philadelphia he took another train and arrived in New York on Tuesday morning, September 4, 1838. Freedom! "When I get to heaven, gon' put on my shoes and gon' walk all over God's heaven . . ."

Frederick didn't know anyone. He had no money, no food, no place to sleep. But, he was on free soil! Since 1827 all New York slaves had been free under the New York Emancipation Act. As he had been instructed, Frederick found the home of David Ruggles, a conductor on the Underground Railroad.

The Underground Railroad was the term given to a network of antislavery sympathizers who secretly, and at great personal risk, helped runaway slaves. They provided food, clothing, and shelter at rest points called "stations." At each station the runaway was told where to find the next stop on the railroad. In this way, step by step, mile after mile, hundreds of slaves inched their way to freedom. The underground workers, called "conductors," also helped runaways find other family members, secure jobs, and set up housekeeping once they reached freedom.

The first thing Frederick did was send an important message to Anna Murray. Just as they had vowed to each other, Anna rushed to New York. They were married immediately.

The bride and groom had no money, but they had each other and their freedom! They had the security of knowing that no man could separate them by selling one away from the other. They had the simple pleasure of knowing that their children would be theirs and no one's "property." Frederick was young and strong. He knew, if given half a chance, that he could be a good provider. But no amount of money in the world could replace the joy of being free! For the moment, that was enough to keep him going.

Ruggles told Frederick about the whaling ships that were refitted in New Bedford, Massachusetts. First-rate caulkers were always needed. Ruggles helped Frederick and his bride of one day to board a steamer to New Bedford. Once there, they were to contact Mr. Nathan Johnson, the next conductor on the Underground Railroad.

Although Johnson assured Frederick that he was safe in New Bedford, a change of name was suggested. Johnson recently had read Sir Walter Scott's narrative poem *The Lady of the Lake*, and had admired the noble character of the heroine's politically outlawed father, Lord James of Douglas. He suggested that Frederick change his last name to Douglas.

Frederick was a bit reluctant to do so. His beloved mother had named him Frederick Augustus Washington Bailey. From his reading of history he had learned that Frederick, Augustus, and Washington had been great generals. In the end he decided to adopt Johnson's protective suggestion.

When doing so, Frederick added an extra "s" to Douglas. Slaves often made minor changes in the spelling of names that had been associated with white people. This personalized their names and helped to separate them from their slave masters.

Although Frederick Douglass took his new name from a fictional Scottish nobleman, he kept the spirit of the name his mother had given him by becoming a general in the struggle for black freedom and justice in the United States.

With a new name, a new wife, and newly won freedom, Frederick Douglass was ready to face the world. He wrote: "The dreams of my childhood and the purposes of my manhood were now fulfilled. A free state around me, and a free earth under my feet! What a moment was this to me! A whole year was pressed into a single day. A new world burst upon my agitated vision."

Mrs. Sophia Auld teaching Frederick his alphabet

The only time the slaves had free time was on Sundays. They could go to prayer meetings (above) or sit around talking (below), usually about freedom.

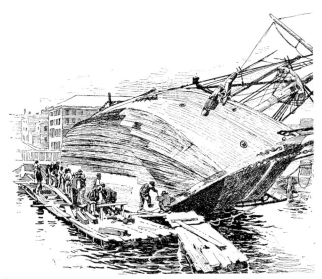

In 1825, Frederick was moved to Baltimore, which was the
largest city in Maryland and a bustling seaport.
He eventually became a caulker in the shipyards.

If discovered, an escaped slave could be seized according to the Fugitive Slave Law.

A meeting of abolitionists in Baltimore

John Brown made an unsuccessful attempt to capture the federal arsenal at Harper's Ferry, Virginia. He was captured, tried, and hanged.

Harriet Tubman helped to lead more than three hundred slaves to freedom on the Underground Railroad.

Nat Turner frightened slave owners when he rebelled and killed his master and his family and others.

Harriet Beecher Stowe's book, *Uncle Tom's Cabin,* helped to destroy the institution of slavery.

William Lloyd Garrison in the office of *The Liberator*

Black soldiers in action in the Civil War

The 55th Massachusetts Regiment, one of the two black regiments raised in 1863 to fight in the Civil War.

Frederick Douglass, then serving as marshal of the District of Columbia, attends the inauguration of President Garfield.

Douglass's house in Washington, D.C.

Chapter 6

THE ABOLITIONIST

> I had been living four or five months in New
> Bedford when there came a young man to me
> with a copy of the *Liberator*, the paper edited
> by William Lloyd Garrison . . . and asked me to
> subscribe for it. . . . From this time I was
> brought into contact with the mind of Mr. Gar-
> rison, and his paper took a place in my heart
> second to the Bible. . . . I loved this paper and
> its editor.

From *Life and Times of Frederick Douglass*
by Frederick Douglass

Frederick loved his new home. New Bedford was very
different from Baltimore and the plantations on the Eastern
Shore. Without slave labor to depend on, northerners had
developed more time-saving devices which, in turn, helped
create more efficient and cost-saving enterprises. What it
took ten or twelve unwilling slaves to do in three hours, an

ox and two men could do in half the time and at a quarter of the cost. Frederick had always believed slavery was morally wrong. After seeing how well northern businesses were managing without slave labor, he was convinced the southern system was an economic disaster.

Frederick was also amazed that free blacks in the area were proud, industrious citizens. All his life he'd been told that black slaves were lazy and ignorant. Seeing the actions of free men in New Bedford helped him appreciate his personal self-worth.

What were the benefits to slaves of hard work in slavery? Very little. In freedom the benefits of hard work were wages and self-respect. Frederick realized that his fellow slaves were not lazy. They deliberately took their time doing work, blundered jobs, and pretended to be stupid. It was their way of sabotaging the system. More than ever, Frederick saw how inefficient was the slavery system.

Douglass believed education made the difference. "I was not long in finding the cause of the difference . . . between the people of the North and South," wrote Douglass. "It was the superiority of educated mind over mere brute force." Many things were becoming clearer. Keep a people ignorant, and they will be forever enslaved. Douglass firmly believed that education was the key to real freedom.

Five days after arriving in New Bedford, Frederick had

gone out to find work. He earned fifty cents for doing a small chore for the minister's wife. It was the first time he had earned money that belonged to him. How wonderful he felt making an "honest" living.

That first free winter was the real test.

For a man who had lived most of his life in a mild climate, his first New England winter was difficult. Frederick and Anna worked together to build a small home. By doing all kinds of odd jobs, the young husband provided food, clothing, and shelter for himself and his wife. Frederick often said that he worked ten times harder for himself than he ever had for a master. He was proud of his accomplishments. So was Anna. What was he capable of doing if given the chance?

In the spring, Douglass looked for work in his trade. It didn't shock him to learn that there was racial prejudice in New Bedford, too. In the North blacks were "free" but not "equal" in the eyes of the law or the local citizens. In many ways there existed rigid racial barriers.

Since he was a caulker, Frederick went to the docks to look for work. He was given a job, but the white workers threatened to leave if a black man were allowed to do skilled work at two dollars a day. There were unemployed white men who needed the work. When all the white men were hired, and there was an extra job, then a black man could be hired. If a layoff was necessary, it was the black man who had to be laid off first. These were the conditions of the "last to be hired and first to be fired" employment system.

Frederick accepted those conditions, and worked as a-dollar-a-day laborer until a caulking position opened for a black man. He was happy to have steady work and be able to take home the full wages from his labors. The working environment wasn't bad, and the men were basically friendly.

During their first year in New Bedford, the Douglasses joined the Methodist Church where they met other blacks who could read and write. They gathered at the black school on Second Street to meet and discuss the issues of the day. It was at one of these local meetings that Frederick learned more about the antislavery movement, and about some of the spokesmen for the cause. It was through one of his friends that he was introduced to the *Liberator*, a newspaper published and edited by William Lloyd Garrison. Frederick was so impressed with the man and his ideas that he became a subscriber and one of Garrison's strongest supporters.

William Lloyd Garrison had begun the *Liberator* in Boston on January 1, 1831, with the motto: "Our country is the world—our countrymen are mankind." The paper was the strongest voice against slavery published at that time.

The word abolition had many definitions, depending upon

who was doing the defining. Some, who called themselves abolitionists, advocated the gradual freeing of slaves so that political stability might be preserved. Others supported a "back to Africa settlement." There were abolition groups who thought slaves should be freed, but not allowed to become United States citizens.

William Lloyd Garrison and his followers attacked slavery as a moral issue. Garrison argued that all slaves should be freed immediately and given full rights as American citizens. Anything contrary to that was unacceptable. On this principle he was unyielding. Not only did Garrison support abolition, he was against the use of alcohol, tobacco, capital punishment, secret fraternal organizations, and imprisonment for debts. He was highly criticized for his liberal position on women's rights, and for allowing women to take part in the American Anti-Slavery Society, which he helped to found in 1833.

Garrison became Douglass's champion. Every week the paper came, and Frederick and Anna read it together. When Garrison came to speak in New Bedford, Frederick went to hear him. It changed both men's lives.

The newspaper publisher was described as "a young man of singularly pleasing countenance, earnest and impressive." Frederick listened as Garrison proclaimed, "Prejudice against color is rebellion against God." It was like a dream.

Never before had Douglass heard a white man defend the cause of black people more eloquently and with more personal conviction. Frederick sat on the edge of his seat taking in every word.

Garrison denounced churches who allowed men to profess Christianity while holding human beings in bondage. He was not a fiery speaker, choosing to deliver his messages calmly and eloquently. For those who held opposite opinions, it was easy to disparage Garrison. But, he was neither mad nor a fanatic. He believed in the equality of mankind. And he wasn't afraid to voice his beliefs. To Frederick Douglass, a former slave, this man was like Moses.

Over the next three years Frederick became the father of two children: a daughter, Rosetta, born June 24, 1839, and a son, Lewis Henry, born October 2, 1840. He worked as a caulker and mastered his trade. He attended all the antislavery meetings held in New Bedford, and spoke to his friends and neighbors when they gathered at the school. Little did Frederick Douglass, or the world, know that he was being prepared for a larger role in the antislavery movement in America—a role that would earn him equal measures of love and hatred.

Chapter 7

FREDERICK DOUGLASS

> At last the apprehended trouble came. People doubted if I had even been a slave. . . . In a little less than four years, therefore, after becoming a public lecturer, I was induced to write out the leading facts connected with my experience in slavery, giving names of persons, places, and dates, thus putting it in the power of any who doubted to ascertain the truth or falsehood of my story. This statement [titled "Narrative of Frederick Douglass"] soon became known in Maryland, and I had reason to believe that an effort would be made to recapture me.

From *Life and Times of Frederick Douglass*
by Frederick Douglass

Frederick rapidly became a well-respected speaker in New Bedford. His delivery was excellent and his command of the English language was equally as impressive. Word spread among the various abolitionist groups that young Frederick Douglass from New Bedford was a dynamic speaker who might enhance their antislavery cause. Douglass didn't know it, but he was being considered for important work.

The summer of 1841 was a busy antislavery time. Garrison and his followers planned a large convention to be held in Nantucket. Much to Frederick's surprise, he was asked to address the group. He accepted the invitation with reservations. He doubted anybody would be interested in what he had to say. But the young black orator left a deep impression on his audience. Frederick admitted later that he was terrified of sitting on stage with William Garrison.

"I had not then dreamed of the possibility of my becoming a public advocate of the cause so deeply imbedded in my heart. It was enough for me to listen, to receive, and applaud the great words of others . . ."

His concerns were eliminated when John A. Collins, a local abolitionist, encouraged him to become a spokesperson for the Massachusetts Anti-Slavery Society. Frederick agreed enthusiastically. So began a new chapter in the life of Frederick Douglass, former slave. And, no one person would be a stronger, more forceful spokesman for the abolitionists.

Douglass spoke firsthand about the evils of slavery, assaulting the system by vividly describing plantation life. He dispelled myths and corrected errors that had become accepted as true. One idea he attacked first was that the slave was happy in his condition.

Frederick Douglass stood before non-sympathetic crowds and eloquently expressed the position of the Garrisonian Abolitionist. Slavery was wrong. Men and women were called to speak against it. Single-handedly, Douglass was responsible for convincing many undecided people to take a stand against the slave system.

By speaking out publicly, Frederick interested some, pleased some, but angered many. Daily he risked losing the freedom he cherished. By law he was a fugitive slave; runaways could be legally apprehended and returned to their masters. Article IV, Section 2 of the U.S. Constitution clearly states this regarding a "fugitive (runaway) slave": "No Person held to Service or Labour in one State, under the Laws thereof, escaping into another, shall, in Consequence of any Law or Regulation therein, be discharged from such Service or Labour, but shall be divided up on Claim of the Party to whom such Service or Labour may be due." By law Frederick could have been returned to Thomas Auld. Knowing this, Douglass still could not be convinced to stop. Neither Anna nor his friends could persuade him to take the safe road—to stop traveling and speaking out.

When his son Frederick, Jr., was born on March 3, 1842,

he went home to be with Anna, but within a few weeks he was back on the road giving antislavery speeches.

Being a former slave made Frederick's presentations more believable. He was an embarrassment to slaveholders who said blacks were uneducable, immoral, lazy, and lacking in any virtues. Frederick Douglass was a contradiction who could not be denied. It was clear that he wasn't going to be silenced. So the proslavery sympathizers tried to discredit him. Rumors were spread that Frederick Douglass had never been a slave. It was said that he was too articulate. How could a slave teach himself to use the language so well?

A heckler in one of Frederick's audiences accused him of making up his stories. At first the accusations were few, and he chose to ignore them. Then, more and more, the lie spread. Frederick Douglass had not been a slave. It would have been humorous had it not been so dreadful.

The problem was that he spoke too well, one of his white advisers said. Perhaps if he sprinkled in some plantation talk. But Frederick refused, arguing that using slave dialect played into the hands of those who said the slave was uneducable, ignorant, and unable to learn like white people. He was living proof that, if given the opportunity, combined with desire and hard work, a black person was as capable of learning as any other.

Another one of his advisers suggested that he try being more humble—more meek. Frederick argued that to be anything other than himself would be lying. He chose instead to write a paper titled "The Narrative of Frederick Douglass." In it he told about his life as a slave using names, places, and dates that could be verified. *Frederick Douglass* had not been a slave. That man was born in New Bedford, September 1838. Frederick Augustus Washington Bailey, son of Harriet Bailey, had been a slave, and everything he said was true. For a while this silenced those who wanted to discredit the antislavery movement by exposing Douglass as a fraud.

In early 1843 the New England Anti-Slavery Society, headed by Garrison, decided to hold a series of one hundred conventions in New Hampshire, Vermont, New York, Ohio, Indiana, and Pennsylvania. Douglass was asked to help.

It was a grueling schedule and an emotionally exhausting venture. In Ohio the convention met with mob violence. They couldn't find a place to hold their meetings, so Frederick had a platform built in a nearby wooded area. There he spoke passionately against slavery. Suddenly, an egg smashed against his chest. Then one hit his head. Still he would not stop speaking.

"I am Frederick Douglass, a former slave . . ." He never got to finish. About forty men attacked him. Frederick and other members of the group were beaten. His hand was broken. Still he would not stop.

When Douglass recovered, he and the group went to Indiana. There the society was greeted more favorably.

At the end of the six-month tour, Douglass was glad to get home to Anna and the children. He was there to greet his new son, Charles, who was born in October 1844.

The following year Frederick expanded his biographical statement and published it as a book entitled *Narrative of the Life of Frederick Douglass*. It was the first of several autobiographies. The book was widely distributed and inevitably reached Baltimore. Word came that the Aulds were trying to get "their property" returned to them. For his own safety he was encouraged to go to Europe. There he would be safe. Reluctantly, he agreed to go abroad.

Chapter 8

THE NORTH STAR

> *The North Star* was a large sheet, published weekly, at a cost of $80 per week, and an average circulation of 3,000 subscribers.

From *Life and Times of Frederick Douglass*
by Frederick Douglass

Accompanied by a young white friend, James M. Buffin, Douglass booked passage on the steamer *Cambia*. His friend was permitted to purchase a cabin ticket, but Frederick was not. Buffin was outraged. Frederick assured him that traveling in steerage would be fine. Blacks were often insulted in this way. Although Douglass never condoned such treatment, he couldn't take the time to fight racial prejudice every time he was confronted with it. He found it useless and very frustrating to argue with day-to-day operations, often run by people who didn't make the decisions in the first place. It was more practical to use his energies working on the legal abolition of discrimination.

When it was learned that *the* Frederick Douglass, the antislavery orator, was on board, he was asked to make a speech before the passengers. He accepted, but two Southerners regarded the invitation as a personal offense. They threatened to throw Douglass off the ship if he dared attempt to speak. Frederick Douglass was not one to back down. He spoke, and he wasn't thrown off the ship.

In England, the incident backfired on the hotheaded young Southerners. The British press denounced their actions and gave the "black American" a sympathetic audience for his antislavery speeches. Frederick and his companions were treated with kindness and respect by the British.

One of the most moving experiences Douglass had while visiting England was to meet Thomas Clarkson, the man who began the antislavery movement in England. Clarkson had helped to make slavery illegal in many parts of the world. When Douglass and William Lloyd Garrison, who was in England at the time, were introduced to Clarkson, the aged antislavery fighter said, "God bless you, Frederick Douglass! I have given sixty years of my life to the emancipation of your people, and if I had sixty years more they should all be given to the same cause." Clarkson was old and the visit was short, but Frederick never forgot this meeting.

In one of his later autobiographies Douglass compared the way he was treated in England to how he was treated in the

United States. "Whatever may be said of the aristocracies here, there is none based on the color of a man's skin. This species of aristocracy belongs preeminently to 'the land of the free, and the home of the brave.' I have never found it abroad in any but Americans. It sticks to them wherever they go. They find it almost as hard to get rid of as to get rid of their skins."

Douglass's stinging words angered some, but they caused others to think. He supported his statement with incidents that actually happened to him when in England. For example, while visiting Eaton Hall, the residence of the Marquis of Westminster, he met several Americans he remembered from the *Cambia*. When they saw that a black man was to be included on the tour, they were visibly upset. Nobody else seemed to notice or care—only the Americans.

Frederick humorously recalled: "I had as much attention paid to me by the servants who showed us through the house as any with a paler skin. As I walked through the building the statuary did not fall down, the pictures did not leap from their places, the doors did not refuse to open, and the servants did not say, '*We don't allow niggers in here.*'"

While in partial exile, Douglass spent most of his time lecturing in many of the principal European cities, raising money to help the antislavery cause in America. He wrote Anna daily, and eagerly awaited her responses detailing the children's lives. The two oldest were reading and writing. The youngest were beginning to spell and count. No father was more proud or more protective of his family than Frederick Douglass. He missed them terribly and longed to return home. But going home was out of the question. It would mean his immediate re-enslavement.

Then quite unexpectedly, two women, Ellen Richardson and Mrs. Henry Richardson bought Frederick's freedom. The transaction was criticized by hard-core Garrisonian abolitionists. They said it was contrary to their doctrine that stated that freedom was a God-given right: Garrisonian abolitionists believed it was impossible to buy or sell a human being.

Frederick saw it differently. He weighed what was against what should have been. According to law, he belonged to Hugh Auld, and could be legally returned to him if Douglass set foot in the United States. Frederick's family was in America. He missed them; they needed him. He studied the problem, asking himself what good he was doing in Europe. The root of his problem was in the United States. That's where he was needed and could do the most good. With his freedom papers purchased by the Richardsons, he could work without fear of being kidnapped and enslaved again. Once his mind was made up, he moved without doubt or apologies.

Frederick Douglass accepted the Richardsons' generous offer. With the stroke of a pen, he was a free man! Thomas Auld sold Frederick to his brother Hugh Auld for $100 on November 13, 1846. The Richardsons paid Hugh Auld for Frederick's freedom on December 5, 1846.

From Europe Douglass wrote Thomas Auld—his old master—the only letter in existence written by a (former) slave to his (former) master. He signed the letter:

I am your fellow-man, but not your slave

So, after three years of living in exile, Frederick returned home in the spring of 1847. He was thirty years old, returning to the United States, ready to take up the battle against slavery again.

This time he would use another vehicle. With $2,500 raised for him by his British friends, Frederick Douglass planned to start an antislavery newspaper. He was unprepared for the overwhelming outrage against his decision. Some of his longtime friends in Boston said a black man could not succeed in publishing a newspaper. But Douglass knew that it was possible. A black newspaper had been published as early as 1827. Blacks had produced textbooks and written novels and poetry. Why couldn't he?

One of his friends from the Anti-Slavery Society argued that Frederick was a good speaker but a former slave with no formal education. He couldn't possibly be an editor. Douglass knew that Garrison had not been formally trained to be an editor. There were many successful, self-taught businessmen. Why couldn't he learn too?

Some of the society members refused to support him publicly. Some supported his efforts privately, but denounced Douglass among their peers for competing against Garrison's paper.

Frederick resented that accusation more than any others. His intent was never to undercut Garrison. Garrison's paper was one voice "crying in the wilderness." Douglass felt his paper would add support to the cause by reinforcing many of Garrison's ideas.

Amidst this controversy, Douglass continued making plans to start a newspaper. He decided to leave New Bedford and relocate his family in Rochester, New York. There, although less well known than he had been in New Bedford, he began his weekly paper in the fall of 1847. Frederick called it *The North Star*, naming it for the star that was the guiding light to freedom for runaway slaves. He thought the name appropriate and meaningful to those who understood its significance.

His new neighbors in Rochester reacted to *The North Star* with mixed opinions. Some felt it was a disgrace for the city to have a "negro paper" in town. Others regarded it as useless and nothing to worry about. But enough people thought it worthy and subscribed to it to keep it in business for one year, then two, and three years and more.

The North Star grew in eight years to serve about three thousand subscribers. Meeting weekly deadlines took total family involvement. Each person had a task and worked at it night and day. Quality was important to Douglass—quality writing, printing, and delivery.

During the first year there was hardly enough money to keep the paper going. With the help of his British friends and other influential people who believed in what he was doing, the paper survived. Frederick—and his family —survived.

On more than one occasion Southerners visited Douglass in Rochester to make sure he was a black man. They refused to believe that he really wrote the newspaper's editorials. However, once a person met Frederick Douglass there was no doubt that he was a black man, and that he had written every word in *The North Star*.

The newspaper became Douglass's voice. He used his editorials to speak out against local racial injustices and, in many cases, helped to bring about a change. One situation he helped to better was the condition of the educational system in Rochester.

The Douglasses believed in education and wanted the best for their children. They felt the Rochester school system was not very good at the time. After hearing about a good private school for girls, Tracy Seminary, Frederick enrolled his nine-year-old daughter, Rosetta. After a few days Rosetta came home crying. Miss Tracy wouldn't allow Rosetta to eat or play with the other girls. In all ways, except in the classroom, Rosetta was segregated. Frederick protested to Miss Tracy, the headmistress. She argued that the other girls would be insulted if Rosetta were to be included in their play and games. Without hesitation, Frederick asked each girl to speak up honestly about how she felt. Not one girl opposed Rosetta's presence. In fact the girls made a point of saying that they didn't mind.

Still, Miss Tracy would not change her position. She insisted that the parents of the other girls should be consulted. They were. All the parents—except one—agreed that Rosetta should be included. Based on one parent's objections, Miss Tracy insisted that Rosetta had to be kept in "isolation." Since Frederick would not permit that, his daughter was withdrawn from the school.

Angrily he wrote: "Of course Miss Tracy was a devout Christian lady after the fashion of the time and locality, in good and regular standing in the church."

Throughout 1848, Frederick fought to desegregate schools in Rochester, writing stinging editorials and making speeches that called for action. After repeated efforts, he accomplished that goal. He also did a great deal to eliminate segregated cars on trains and other public transportation as well.

Douglass never rested in his struggle against slavery, injustice, and racial discrimination. He was not the only black involved in that struggle. Harriet Tubman, one of his fellow Marylanders and also a former slave, was helping to lead more than three hundred slaves to freedom on the Underground Railroad. There was the work of Sojourner Truth, also a former slave. She was illiterate, but she was a forceful speaker. "Not a dry eye [was there] in one of Sojourner Truth's audiences . . ."

There were whites as well who had dedicated their lives to the fight against slavery. One well-known writer, Wendell Phillips, wrote persuasive essays, poems, and pamphlets against slavery. And, there was John Greenleaf Whittier, whose poem Douglass liked to quote:

THE FAREWELL
OF A VIRGINIA SLAVE MOTHER TO HER DAUGHTER, SOLD INTO SOUTHERN BONDAGE

Gone, gone—sold and gone,
To the rice-swamp dank and lone.
Where the slave-whip ceaseless swings,

Where the noisome insect stings,
Where the fever demon strews
Poison with the falling dews,
Where the sickly sunbeams glare
Through the hot and misty air;
    Gone, gone—sold and gone,
    To the rice-swamp dank and lone,
    From Virginia's hills and waters;
    Woe is me, my stolen daughter.

By word and deed, blacks and whites in the United States, Canada, and Europe were rallying to seek an end to slavery.

How to end slavery, and what to do with the freed slaves afterward, were the headlines of the day. Slavery was no longer an issue discussed after dinner, but hotly debated on the floor of the United States Congress. More and more antislavery senators and congressmen were being elected. The abolitionists were making progress in places where it made a difference.

Douglass remained a loyal Garrisonian supporter, advocating that dissolving the Union was the best way to remove "federal protection" from slave states, and that nonviolent persuasion was the best attack against it.

Slowly, however, Douglass's opinions changed. To dissolve the Union—separate the North from the South—would leave slaves at the mercy of the slave owners. He also believed that it would take violence to get the South to release the slaves.

Then in May 1851, the split between Garrison and Douglass finally happened. Frederick spoke at the annual meeting of the American Anti-Slavery Society. There he expressed his new position, and the outcry against him was furious.

Thereafter, *The North Star* was no longer an approved abolitionist newspaper. Frederick wrote about that time: "This radical change in my opinions produced a corresponding change in my action. To those [with] whom I had been in agreement, I came to be in opposition."

Frederick Douglass still admired William Lloyd Garrison. But, he disagreed with his friend on many points. Evidence shows that Douglass didn't want their long relationship to end bitterly. He wrote to Charles Sumner, another leader among the abolitionists, saying that his relationship to Garrison was something like a child to a parent. But, Douglass stopped short of changing his attitude. He had his beliefs and he wasn't going to change them. So he remained an outcast.

Garrison never made a public statement regarding Douglass, but he was reported to have said privately that Douglass was destitute of every principle of honor, ungrateful to the last degree, unworthy of respect, confidence or countenance.

Frederick responded, claiming Garrison's followers were no more than "mental slaves" and "vigilant enemies." He wrote in *The North Star*: "They act as though . . . all Anti-Slavery ideas originated with them and that no man has a right to 'peep or mutter' on the subject, who does not hold letters patent from them." Meanwhile, the proslavery groups were glad to see a rip in the antislavery quilt. For a while it weakened their cause.

The next ten years would prove to be very trying for Frederick Douglass as an abolitionist, a person, and as a citizen of the United States.

Chapter 9

JOHN BROWN

> If I have at any time said or written that which is worth remembering or repeating, I must have said such things between the years 1848 to 1860 . . . within that space we had . . . the Fugitive-Slave Law . . . the Dred Scott decision, the repeal of the Missouri Compromise, the Kansas Nebraska bill, the Border War in Kansas, the John Brown raid upon Harper's Ferry . . .

From *Life and Times of Frederick Douglass*
by Frederick Douglass

In 1850 the country was in turmoil over the expansion of slavery into the western territories. After the War of 1812, pioneers left the eastern states and had begun moving west. New states had been admitted to the Union regularly, and without controversy. By 1819 there were twenty-two states: eleven were slave states, and eleven were free states. There was equal representation in Congress.

In that same year Missouri applied for statehood as a slave state. Antislavery advocates argued that admitting Missouri as a slave state would open up slavery to the lands in the Louisiana Purchase. Proslavery advocates, mostly Southerners, counterargued that the people of each state had a right to choose slavery or not.

However, Maine also applied for admission to the Union in 1819. There was a compromise. Missouri was admitted as a slave state, and Maine was admitted as a free state. Congress stayed balanced. But another agreement was reached as well. A line was drawn along the 36 degree parallel in the lands of the Louisiana Purchase (referred to as the Mason-Dixon Line). North of the line, slavery was not permitted. South of the line, Congress would not pass laws against it. These were the terms of the Missouri Compromise, and so the matter stayed for some thirty years.

But in 1850, the tension between slave states and free states was mounting again. Slaves were running away, many with the assistance of the Underground Railroad. Abolitionists called for the immediate removal of slavery from every state. Southerners angrily responded that Northerners were interfering with their way of life. They accused Northern industrialists of inflaming the problem to gain control of the country.

Throughout the 1840s Douglass had used *The North Star*

to report these events. The method of that time seemed to be compromise. California was admitted to the Union as a free state, but a stricter fugitive slave law was passed. Bounty hunters came into the North, seized blacks who had been free and forcefully enslaved them. Many free blacks fled into Canada. Anyone caught helping a runaway slave would be fined or jailed. Southern slave owners were happy with the new tougher law. Northerners disobeyed it. Many policemen refused to arrest blacks and return them to the South.

The Douglass house remained an important station along the Underground Railroad. Rochester, New York, located just across from the Canadian border, was the perfect place for slaves to rest and prepare for their final trek to freedom.

Responding to the Fugitive Slave Law, Frederick delivered one of his strongest antislavery speeches in Rochester on December 8, 1850. The title was "The Inhumanity of Slavery." Here is an excerpt from that famous speech:

> We have heard much of late of the virtue of patriotism, the love of country . . . I, too, would invoke the spirit of patriotism; not in a narrow and restricted sense, but, I trust, with a broad and manly signification; not to cover up our national sins, but to inspire us with sincere repentance; not to hide our shame from the

world's gaze, but utterly to abolish the cause of that shame; not to explain away our gross inconsistencies as a nation, but to remove the hateful, jarring, and incongruous elements from the land; not to sustain an egregious wrong, but to unite all our energies in the grand effort to remedy that wrong.

Antislavery passions were stirred deeply by the publication of Harriet Beecher Stowe's *Uncle Tom's Cabin.* Appearing in March 1852, it was an instant literary success selling 300,000 copies in the first year. That one book did as much to destroy the institution of slavery as any other single event. Many scholars list *Uncle Tom's Cabin* as one of the four books that have shaped mankind's destiny.

Frederick Douglass read Mrs. Stowe's book with interest. When he read about Uncle Tom, Little Liza, and the other characters in the story, Frederick was deeply moved. He understood the cruelty of Simon Legree. That Mrs. Stowe had never been in the South was not questioned by her readers. The fictional account was taken as total fact.

Douglass had this to say about the book and the author: "No book on the subject of slavery had so generally and favorably touched the American heart. It combined all the power and pathos of preceding publications of the kind, and was hailed by many as an inspired production."

Mrs. Stowe invited Douglass to her home in Andover, Massachusetts, before she went to England on a publicity tour. She wanted to know Douglass's opinion about a project she had in mind. With money she earned during her European tour, which she estimated would be a large sum, Mrs. Stowe intended to open an industrial school for free blacks who sought to better themselves.

Frederick later wrote: "I lost no time in making my way to Andover. I was received at her home with genuine cordiality. There was no contradiction between the author and her book."

Douglass knew that many blacks who escaped from slavery were unable to care for themselves in the industrial North. They lacked marketable skills. He suggested this to Mrs. Stowe: "What I thought of as best was rather a series of workshops, where colored people could learn some of the handicrafts, learn to work in iron, wood, and leather, and where a plain English education could also be taught. I argued that the want of money was the root of all evil to the colored people. They were shut out from all lucrative employments . . . Their poverty kept them ignorant and their ignorance kept them degraded."

Mrs. Stowe agreed with Douglass. She went to Europe. He returned to Rochester and announced to the black community that Mrs. Stowe was planning to sponsor a manual labor school for free black people. However, when Mrs. Stowe returned to the United States, she had changed her mind about the school. Her reasons were never made public, but she remained a staunch supporter of the antislavery movement. The much-needed school was not opened then, but Frederick didn't give up on the idea.

On July 5, 1852, Frederick was asked to speak at an Independence Day celebration. His subject was: "What to the Slave is the Fourth of July?" Douglass was fired up for the occasion, saying:

> Fellow-Citizens—Pardon me, and allow me to ask, why am I called upon to speak here to-day? What have I, or those I represent, to do with your national independence?
>
> . . . I fancy I hear some of my audience say, it is just in this circumstance that you and your brother abolitionists fail to make a favorable impression on the public mind. Would you agree more, and denounce less, would you persuade more and rebuke less, your cause would be much more likely to succeed. But, I submit, where all is plain there is nothing to be argued. . . . On what branch of the subject do the people

of this country light? Must I undertake to prove that the slave is a man? That point is conceded already. Nobody doubts it. The slaveholders themselves acknowledge it in the enactment of laws for their government. They acknowledge it when they punish disobedience on the part of the slave. There are seventy-two crimes in the state of Virginia, which, if committed by a black man (no matter how ignorant he be), subject him to the punishment of death: while only two of these same crimes will subject a white man to the like punishment. What is this but the acknowledgment that the slave is a moral, intellectual, and responsible being. The manhood of the slave is conceded.

In 1854 Stephen A. Douglas, senator from Illinois, sponsored the Kansas-Nebraska Act. He suggested that when it came time for Kansas and Nebraska to file for statehood, each should be allowed to choose whether it would be a slave or free state. That lifted the barrier established by the Missouri Compromise in 1820. There were heated debates both pro and con. But the Kansas-Nebraska Act passed. Tempers flared. Angry words were exchanged.

Nebraska had firmly decided to be a free state. Kansas

was unsure. A general vote would decide the position Kansas would take. To persuade Kansans to vote their way, Missouri sent a group of proslavery supporters into Kansas. They threatened small isolated farmers. New England antislavery groups sent rifles and men to "protect" the people of Kansas. In truth, the people of Kansas didn't want either side disrupting their lives. Unfortunately, Kansas became the first battleground of the war to come.

One man who went into Kansas on the side of the antislavery fighters was John Brown. Brown was a friend of Frederick Douglass, and influenced Douglass's political position more than any other person except Garrison. He was a regular visitor in the Douglass home. Brown was extremely fond of little Annie, Douglass's youngest daughter.

Brown is generally portrayed as a man feverishly driven, with crazed, glaring eyes, full of rage and righteous indignation. As an antislavery speaker he was quite animated. But he wasn't very different from other speakers of that time. He used the forceful clenched fist, the accusing pointed finger, and the Bible raised overhead. His personal conviction that slavery was wrong was firm, and he was intolerant of anyone who differed with him on this point. Douglass and Brown spent many hours talking. The two men became friends as well as crusaders against slavery. They confided in each other. Frederick shared many stories about his life as a slave with Brown. His friend sat quietly, listening to every word. Brown shared some of his early life with Douglass.

John Brown was born May 9, 1800 at Torrington, Connecticut. He was the grandson of Captain John Brown who served in the Revolutionary War. In 1805 Brown went to live in Hudson, Ohio. At age eighteen he studied for the ministry, but turned to land surveying instead. He soon went bankrupt. He moved to North Elba, New York, and worked on a small tract of land rented to him by Gerrit Smith. Smith was also a leading abolitionist who gave small tracts of land to Negro settlers to get a fresh beginning. Brown told Douglass he had hated slavery from childhood, and believed it to be an abomination against God.

In 1857 the antislavery movement received a crushing blow. Dred Scott, a slave, had lived in a free state. He sued his master for his freedom, stating that he had lived in a free state and was therefore free. The case was taken to the Supreme Court. Justice Roger Brooke Taney ruled against Dred Scott, saying black men were not U.S. citizens and therefore could not take a case to court. "Negroes . . . have no rights which the white man is bound to respect."

Douglass responded angrily saying the Supreme Court was not the only power in the world. Douglass warned that antislavery fighters weren't going to give up. After the

Supreme Court decision, Dred Scott was freed by the man who had bought him from his original owner.

Kansas was now a battle-torn state. In 1858 John Brown and five of his sons joined the Kansas Border War. He led a group that killed five Southern settlers in retaliation for the burning of Lawrence, Kansas, by some border ruffians. Brown believed the only way to end the slavery issue was through violence. Douglass still held that violence was not the answer. However, he knew war was inevitable.

Brown shared a nonviolent idea with Frederick. Brown wanted to help slaves establish a stronghold in Virginia from where they could strike at the Southern states. "I know these mountains well," he said, "and could take a body of men into them and keep them there despite of all the efforts of Virginia to dislodge them." Brown went on to describe his plan to build a fortress in the Virginia mountains. Any runaway who could make it there would be free to choose to stay and fight, or to work his way through the mountains to freedom. The idea was agreed upon. Frederick and other abolitionists began secretly raising money for that cause.

Shields Green was a runaway from Charleston, South Carolina, and one of Frederick's best friends. Douglass thought it right that his two friends should meet each other. Green became one of Brown's strongest supporters. Then, in the summer of 1859, Douglass met with his two friends to discuss a new plan Brown had in mind. The meeting was held in secret and they were all in disguise.

Brown no longer wanted to build a fortress in the mountains to help slaves escape. Brown's new plan was to capture the arsenal at Harper's Ferry, which was federal property. "Harper's Ferry would serve notice to the slaves that their friends had come, and as a trumpet to rally them . . ." said Brown.

Their talk was long. Douglass was against Brown's idea to capture the arsenal at Harper's Ferry, Virginia. He felt it would be fatal. He tried to reason with Brown, but it was useless. Brown argued that the slaves in the surrounding area would rally around him, and they could take Virginia. Douglass could not go along with Brown's new plan.

Douglass argued as best he could, but in the end there was no way he could convince Brown not to implement his plan. Brown begged Douglass to go with him. It was a painful decision, but Douglass refused. Shields Green went. Douglass knew he would see neither of his friends alive again.

John Brown slipped into Harper's Ferry, Virginia, site of a federal arsenal. On October 16, 1859, with a small band of men, five of whom were black, he captured the arsenal and took six hundred citizens as hostages.

Brown and his followers were counterattacked by a force of United States Marines under the command of Colonel

Robert E. Lee. Brown was wounded. He surrendered. Ten of his men were killed—Shields Green was one of them. Seven were taken as prisoners and five escaped. On the other side five were killed and nine wounded.

Brown was jailed, quickly tried, and convicted of treason and "conspiring and advising with slaves and other rebels and murder in the first degree." On December 2, 1859 he was hanged at Charlestown, Virginia. Of the five blacks who were involved, only one survived.

Southerners portrayed John Brown as a fanatic. Northerners made him a hero. Frederick Douglass did as much as anyone to make him one. The "John Brown Song" almost replaced "Yankee Doodle" in popularity. Brown was made the martyr for the antislavery cause. In death, Brown's fiery voice could still be heard. "What he lost by the sword, he gained by the truth," wrote Frederick Douglass. When rumors spread that Brown had stopped to kiss a black child on the way to the gallows, Douglass said that such an action was in his friend's nature.

Even though there was no evidence against Douglass, the state of Virginia issued a warrant for his arrest. Frederick was advised to leave the country for his own safety. If he stayed he could be indicted as a conspirator in the John Brown incident.

After a few short months in England, Frederick returned

to the United States when word came that his youngest daughter, Annie, had died. For Douglass, the death of his daughter was a terrible loss. He loved his children dearly and protected them. In a letter written to Thomas Auld, he reveals the fatherly pride and love he had for his children:

> So far as my domestic affairs are concerned, I can boast of as comfortable a dwelling as your own. I have an industrious and neat companion, and four dear children—the oldest a girl of nine years, and three fine boys, the oldest eight, the next six, and the youngest four years old. [Annie had not been born when this letter was written.] The three oldest are now going regularly to school—two can read and write, and the other can spell, with tolerable correctness, words of two syllables . . . They are all in comfortable beds, and are sound asleep, perfectly secure under my own roof. There are no slaveholders here to rend my heart by snatching them from my arms. . . .

But there is no defense against death. Death had snatched his baby daughter from his arms. He could not be comforted. ". . . The light of my life had gone out," he wrote.

Douglass never really got over the death of little Annie. He spoke of her often throughout his life.

The decade had ended. The country was ripping apart along the Mason-Dixon Line. It was 1860—an election year.

Chapter 10

ABRAHAM LINCOLN

> (Lincoln) . . . alone of all our Presidents was to
> have the opportunity to destroy slavery and lift
> into manhood millions of his countrymen hith-
> erto held as chattels and numbered with the
> beasts of the field.

From *Life and Times of Frederick Douglass*
by Frederick Douglass

There were three candidates for the presidency of the
United States in 1860. The Democratic party was divided.
Senator Stephen A. Douglas from Illinois represented the
western faction. John C. Breckenridge was the slaveholders'
candidate. Illinois lawyer Abraham Lincoln represented the
united Republican party. The Republicans considered slavery a moral, social, and political evil. Naturally, they had the
support of the various antislavery groups.

Stephen Douglas argued that it was up to each state to
choose whether slavery should or should not be accepted,

and it was not up to the federal government to legislate that issue.

Breckenridge believed slavery was legal anywhere a slaveholder chose to take his slaves. If a man from Georgia moved to New York, he should be able to hold slaves in New York, just as he had in Georgia. Those in New York who didn't want to hold slaves would not be forced to do so. And, at least in principle, the Supreme Court agreed with Breckenridge, with its decision in the Dred Scott case.

Abraham Lincoln strongly disagreed with both candidates, stating:

> . . . In my opinion, it will cease until a crisis shall have been reached and passed. "A house divided against itself cannot stand." I believe this government cannot endure permanently half slave and half free. I do not expect the Union to be dissolved; I do not expect the house to fall; but I do expect it will cease to be divided. It will become all one thing or all the other. Either the opponents of slavery will arrest the further spread of it, and place it where the public mind shall rest in the belief that it is in the course of ultimate extinction, or its advocates will push it forward till it shall

become alike lawful in all the States, old as well as new, North as well as South.

... Power ought to be exercised to the extent of confining slavery inside the slave states, with a view of ultimate extinction.

Lincoln's statement infuriated slaveholders. Led by South Carolina, the South threatened to withdraw from the Union if Breckenridge were not elected. Some thought South Carolina was bluffing. Others knew the threat was very real. Compromise and moderation were terms widely used. New York businessmen were the first to call for compromise. Northern manufacturers needed the trade from the South. To them slavery was a secondary issue. Economics dictated their politics.

Amid the political turmoil Abraham Lincoln was elected sixteenth president of the United States in November 1860 at age fifty-one. Although he didn't rush right in and free the slaves as many thought he would, his election was enough; South Carolina seceded from the Union on December 20, 1860, to be followed soon by Georgia, Louisiana, Mississippi, Florida, Alabama, and Texas.

Antislavery meetings in the North were attacked. Many deserted the cause since it seemed almost un-American to be part of a group that was responsible for destroying the

Union. Douglass called the desertions "misguided patriotism." His voice could be heard above all those who were counseling moderation. His plea was for no compromise when it came to the rights and freedom of the slave.

In frustration, Douglass and a few other black leaders discussed the possibility of colonizing blacks in Haiti. Even Lincoln favored the idea.

Then, on April 12, 1861, the seven seceded states, now united as the Confederate States of America, fired on federal troops at Fort Sumter, South Carolina. Four more states—Arkansas, North Carolina, Virginia, and Tennessee—also joined the Confederacy. Jefferson Davis, who had resigned his seat as United States senator from Mississippi in January 1861, was elected president of the Confederate States of America. The war was on.

Several slaveholding states in the Union, Kentucky, Maryland, and Missouri, were among them. It was truly a divided country. Brothers within the same family chose to fight on opposite sides. Husbands and wives were divided, and fathers and sons. Even in New York there had been talk that the state would secede with South Carolina in order to maintain trade. New York didn't leave the Union, but there were many Northerners who sympathized with the South. They were called "Copperheads."

Frederick Douglass watched the war from his Rochester

home, writing and speaking as he had for years. He was deeply concerned that Lincoln wouldn't free the slaves. Freedmen weren't allowed to fight for the Union. After a full two years into the war, things hadn't changed much for the slave. Northern generals warned that if slaves took up arms against their masters they would be dealt with severely. Yet one Union officer declared the slaves in Missouri free. Lincoln invalidated the order. Blacks tried to enlist in the Union army, but were refused. Still the Union continued to send fugitive slaves back to the South.

Finally, on January 1, 1863, at approximately 11:00 P.M., Abraham Lincoln signed the Emancipation Proclamation, freeing the slaves. The words were simple and very direct:

> . . . all persons held as slaves within any State
> or designated part of a State, the people where-
> of shall then be in rebellion against the United
> States, shall be thenceforth and forever free.

Boston celebrated wildly, and Frederick Douglass was one of the principal speakers on that occasion. There were cries of joy, and hugs of relief. The long, hard battle had been won. But Douglass knew the battle had really just begun. Along with freedom must come justice. And right away Frederick began to work on justice.

Slavery was outlawed only in the seceding states. In the border states—slave states that stayed in the Union—slavery was still legal. There were 800,000 slaves within the Union. Douglass was very instrumental in getting this issue brought before the public. He wrote letter after letter to Secretary of War Edwin M. Stanton, urging the enlistment of blacks. Finally, he was given an opportunity to present his case to Secretary Stanton. The War Department initiated the Bureau of Colored Troops.

On March 2, 1863, Massachusetts raised two black regiments, the 54th and 55th. Frederick's sons, Charles and Lewis, were among the first to enlist. Douglass used *The North Star* and his persuasive oratory to get blacks to join the army, saying: "Liberty won by white men would lose half its luster. 'Who would be free, themselves must strike the blow. Better even die free, than to live slaves.'"

White officers were not pleased with the decision to use black soldiers. Some openly refused to serve with black men. But Lincoln and his advisers held fast to their decision. Black soldiers fought honorably for the Union. They were in the front lines of several battles: the battle of Nashville, Milliken's Bend, Point Lookout, and Fort Wagner, where the Massachusetts 54th distinguished itself.

Frederick Douglass was disturbed about the treatment of black soldiers. They were not paid equally; they were not protected when taken prisoner; and they were not promoted or given honors.

Douglass was allowed to meet President Lincoln to express his concerns. It was one of the greatest honors ever given a black man at the time.

On the subject of equal pay, Douglass told the president about the 54th Massachusetts Volunteers, the regiment he had helped to raise. They had protested for nearly a year about the seven dollars' pay they were given in contrast to the thirteen dollars white soldiers were paid. Yet, Douglass stated, the black soldiers of the 54th had marched on Fort Wagner in South Carolina and succeeded in entering the fort in the face of heavy fire. Was it fair that such gallantry be rewarded with less pay?

Douglass presented to the president his opinion regarding soldiers being protected. The South refused to recognize the black soldier as having the same rights as a white prisoner of war. In fact blacks caught or wounded were usually killed.

On the matter of awards and promotions, Douglass pointed out that of the 7,122 officers in the Union army, there were only 75 black officers. Black soldiers were not recognized for their outstanding contributions in the war.

Lincoln listened patiently while Douglass expressed his three concerns. At the end, Lincoln responded that on the first two issues, he could not move immediately. On the last issue, Lincoln promised he would recommend that black soldiers be justly rewarded.

At the close of the historic meeting, Lincoln thanked Frederick Douglass for coming. He promised to do what he could to help. Douglass wondered if his meeting had done any good. It had.

By January 1, 1864, Congress voted equal pay to black soldiers. Thirteen black soldiers were awarded the Congressional Medal of Honor and six received the Navy Medal of Honor. More than 186,000 black soldiers served in the Union army during the Civil War: 38,000 died.

Much to Frederick's delight, Lincoln was reelected for a second term. The war ended when on April 9, 1865, General Lee surrendered to General Grant at Appomattox. On the night of April 14, 1865, Lincoln was shot. He died early the next morning.

The country mourned. Frederick Douglass wrote that he—and all black men—had lost a true friend. Mrs. Lincoln sent one of Lincoln's walking sticks to Frederick with a note: "My husband often spoke of sending you a gift of friendship." Douglass counted the walking stick as one of his personal treasures.

The Civil War was over, but it had taken its toll. Thousands of young blacks and whites had died. Whether or not the war had been fought because of slavery seemed unimportant in the wake of human disaster. Blacks were free at last, but free to do what? They had no jobs, no skills, no money, and no education.

Frederick Douglass spent many hours speaking out for ratification of the Thirteenth Amendment. It passed in 1865, and all slavery ended in the United States.

Led by Senator Sumner, the Civil Rights Act of 1866 gave all slaves citizenship and the Fourteenth Amendment gave all male blacks the right to vote. In March 1870, the Fifteenth Amendment, protecting the black's right to vote, was passed. It was the black votes that helped to elect President Ulysses S. Grant in 1868.

The 1870s were a hopeful time for blacks. Frederick Douglass, the "Black Lion," had been fighting for so very long. Slavery had been abolished in the United States. Frederick felt satisfied that his work was complete. Anna thought it time for him to take a much-needed rest. His children were grown and married. They encouraged him to slow down. Douglass agreed. He closed *The North Star* and began working on personal projects for which he had not had time. He was in his early fifties.

Chapter 11

THE GOLDEN YEARS

I have sometimes been credited with having been the architect of my own fortune, and have pretty generally received the title of a "self-made man," and while I cannot altogether disclaim this title, when I look back over the facts of my life, and consider the helpful influences exerted upon me, by friends and those more fortunately born and educated than myself, I am compelled to give them at least an equal measure of credit, with myself, for the success which has attended my labors in life.

From *Life and Times of Frederick Douglass*
by Frederick Douglass

In his own words, Douglass said his life was very busy between 1870 and 1880. He visited Santo Domingo, was appointed a council member for the government of the District of Columbia, and appointed by President Rutherford

B. Hayes to the office of marshal of the District of Columbia.

After selling *The North Star*, the Douglasses sold their house in Rochester and moved to Washington, D.C. They bought a house in Anacostia on a hill overlooking the Capitol. They called it Cedar Hill. And, for a time, Douglass was content to enjoy his grandchildren.

But not for long. Frederick Douglass was still a popular spokesperson for black Americans. One of the greatest speeches he delivered during this time was at the unveiling of the Lincoln Monument. Both houses of Congress were closed so that members could attend the ceremony. On April 14, 1876, he made one of his most impressive speeches. Newspaper accounts indicated that the audience was very quiet and attentive. No one seemed to mind that the speech was an hour and a half long.

When President Hayes appointed Douglass marshal of the District of Columbia, Frederick "provoked something like a scream—I will not say a *yell*—of popular displeasure." Douglass went on to explain: "[They thought] I would surround myself with colored deputies, colored bailiffs, and colored messengers and pack the jury-box with colored jurors—in a word, Africanize the courts."

Douglass believed that the real cause for concern was age-old bigotry. "But the most dreadful thing threatened was a colored man at the *Executive Mansion* in white kid gloves, sparrow-tailed coat, patent-leather boots, and alabaster cravat, performing the ceremony—a very empty one—of introducing the aristocratic citizens of the republic to the President of the United States. This was something entirely too much to be borne, and men asked themselves in view of it, 'To what is the world coming? and where will these things stop?' Dreadful! Dreadful!"

During the time that Douglass was marshal he went to visit his old master, Thomas Auld, at St. Michaels in Talbot County, Maryland. Douglass had gone there to see a friend, when a message arrived from Auld asking him to visit. The former slave master was past eighty and on his deathbed.

Frederick accepted the invitation. It made international news. Arriving at the front door as a guest, he couldn't help but think how many things had changed. Douglass was taken to the dying man's bedroom. He described it this way:

> We addressed each other simultaneously, he calling me "Marshal Douglass," and I, as I had always called him, "Captain Auld." . . . I instantly broke up the formal nature of the meeting by saying, "not *Marshal*, but Frederick to you as formerly." We shook hands cordially, and in the act of doing so, he, having been long stricken with palsy, shed tears as

men thus afflicted will do when excited by any deep emotion. . . . We both . . . got the better of our feelings, and conversed freely about the past.

Auld was asked what he thought about Douglass's running away when still a slave. Thomas Auld answered that under the same circumstances he would have done the same thing.

Frederick was able to get the record straight about his grandmother, Betsey Bailey. In one of his earlier biographies, Frederick had said Auld had left her to die alone and without care. Thomas Auld told Frederick that Grandmama Betsey belonged to his brother-in-law, and that he had sent for her and had taken care of her until she'd died.

While in his old home place, Frederick went to the Lloyd plantation where he had lived many years before. There he met a relative of Colonel Edward Lloyd. Finally, he visited Harper's Ferry where his old friend John Brown had made his desperate stand against slavery. Going "down home" after all those years helped to remove all the bitterness inside Frederick Douglass. He no longer felt the need to hate, only the relief that it was finally over.

But the troubles weren't over. Rutherford B. Hayes had made concessions to the South in order to get the electoral votes he needed to win the close election. He gave each state the right "to control their own affairs in their own way." That meant each state could decide what to do about the "black problem." With states' rights there came "Jim Crow" laws. Everywhere blacks were losing their basic civil rights and constitutional freedom—especially in the South.

Although Douglass was as outspoken as ever against these injustices, he worked for Hayes. It was assumed that he agreed with the states' rights position. Douglass's popularity declined. To many well-educated young blacks, some of whom had been born free, Frederick Douglass was a tool of the establishment. His voice was no longer considered the "roar of the masses." Fewer people—black or white—were listening to him. They were turning instead to another younger black leader rising to power, Booker T. Washington, the Alabama educator.

Douglass's latest edition of his autobiography was attacked by a few disenchanted followers. In a new chapter, Douglass described the joy with which he had received Amanda Auld Sears, the daughter of Miss Lucretia Auld. He wrote:

Amanda made haste to tell me that she agreed with me about slavery, and that she had freed all her slaves as they had become of age. She brought her children to me, and I took them in my arms . . . Mrs. Sears died three years ago in Baltimore, but she did not depart without calling me to her bedside, that I might tell her as much as I could about her mother . . . I told her that the young lady standing in the corner of the room was the image of her mother in form and features. She looked at her daughter and said, "Her name is Lucretia—after my mother." . . . The interview touched me deeply, and was, I could not help thinking, a strange one—another proof that "truth is often stranger than fiction."

If any reader of this part of my life shall see in it the evidence of a want of manly resentment for wrongs inflicted by slavery upon myself and race, and by the ancestors of this lady, so it must be. No man can be stronger than nature, one touch of which, we are told, makes all the world akin.

After serving as marshal of the District of Columbia, Douglass was made recorder of deeds by President Garfield. He held the office for nearly five years, and set an example for the country by showing that a black man could hold public office responsibly.

In the summer of 1882, Anna died. The Douglasses had

been married for over forty years. Anna had not been one to seek public attention, yet Frederick received hundreds of condolence letters. Anna had provided the stability in the home when the children were young; she had worked alongside her husband in the newspaper, and had waited, worried, and rejoiced with him for a good portion of her life. Frederick loved Anna, and there was no doubt that she loved him. Her death left a void in his life. Cedar Hill was not the same without her gentle comforting voice.

Then in 1884, Douglass married a white woman, Helen Pitts. The public outcry against the marriage, among both blacks and whites, was unprecedented. In a biography written by Booker T. Washington, Douglass was blasted for taking a white wife. As was his custom, he didn't back down even though popular opinion was against him. Douglass had this to say about his interracial marriage:

> People who remained silent over the unlawful relations of the white slave masters with their colored slave women loudly condemned me for marrying a wife a few shades lighter than myself. They would have had no objection to my marrying a person much darker in complexion than myself, but to marry one much lighter, and of the complexion of my father

rather than that of my mother, was, in the popular eye, a shocking offence . . .

In this statement, Douglass admits for the first time that his father was white. There have been speculations, then and now, that Captain Aaron Anthony was his father; however, there is no positive proof to support this assertion. Throughout his earlier biographical accounts he denies knowing who was his father. However, this statement suggests that he did know.

President Harrison appointed Frederick to the office of minister resident and consul general to the Republic of Haiti. No foreign minister at that time was black. And, once again, he was before the public eye.

He was by this time weary, but still able to take on a good battle. He wrote:

> Neither my character nor my color was acceptable to the New York press. The fault of my character was that upon it there could be predicated no well grounded hope that I would allow myself to be used or allow my office to be used, to further selfish schemes of any sort for the benefit of individuals, either at the expense of Haiti or at the expense of the character of the

United States. And the fault of my color was that it was a shade too dark for American taste.
. . . although I matched well with the color of Haiti.

His years in Haiti were riddled with confusion and bad press. Douglass had fallen out of favor. He was old and, following good counsel, he retired after serving two years.

At Cedar Hill he was surrounded by grandchildren and great-grandchildren. He called these the "golden years."

Later pictures show Douglass with a stone-chiseled face. His white hair feathered around his face like the mane of a great lion. In later years he had been called the "Black Lion." But those who knew Frederick Douglass well took delight in his wonderful sense of humor, his quick smile, charming wit, and his loving and kind ways. When Cedar Hill was full of cheerful voices, he would pull out his violin, which he had taught himself to play years earlier, and fiddle a happy tune. He enjoyed singing, dancing, and reciting poetry. Except for an occasional speaking engagement, he spent his last years at home, collecting and organizing his papers, reading and always writing, up to the end.

He was so robust, no one knew he was sick. But in the winter of 1895, at the age of seventy-eight, Frederick Douglass died. The "Black Lion" would roar no more.

Frederick Douglass 1817-1895

1817 Frederick Augustus Washington Bailey is born a slave.

1820 Missouri Compromise—Maine enters Union as free state and Missouri as slave state. Washington Colonization Society founds Liberia for repatriation of Negroes.

1823 Frederick Augustus Washington Bailey goes to the Lloyd plantation to live on the Thomas Auld farm.

1825 Frederick Augustus Washington Bailey becomes the property of Hugh Auld in Baltimore.

1829 Andrew Jackson inaugurated as seventh president of the U.S.

1831 William Lloyd Garrison begins publishing the abolitionist periodical *The Liberator* in Boston. A slave insurrection at Southampton, Virginia, is led by Negro Nat Turner.

1832 The New England Anti-Slavery Society is founded in Boston.

1834 Frederick Augustus Washington Bailey is delivered to Edward Covey's farm as a slave.

1838 Frederick Augustus Washington Bailey escapes to freedom, marries Anna Murray, takes the name Frederick Douglass, and goes to work in New Bedford.

1839 Rosetta Douglass is born on June 24.

1840 Lewis Henry Douglass is born on October 2.

1842 Frederick Douglass, Jr. is born on March 3.

1844 Charles Remond Douglass is born on October 24.

1845 *Narrative of the Life of Frederick Douglass* is written. Douglass sails for Europe to give antislavery speeches and raise money for the cause in America.

1846 Frederick Douglass's freedom is bought by the Richardsons.

1847 Frederick Douglass returns to the U.S. and begins publication of the antislavery newspaper, *The North Star.* Liberia is proclaimed an independent republic.

1848 Frederick Douglass tries to desegregate the schools in Rochester, New York.

1849 Annie Douglass is born on March 22.

1850 Henry Clay's compromise slavery resolutions are laid before the U.S. Senate. The population of U.S. (23 million) includes 3.2 million black slaves.

1851 Frederick Douglass speaks in Rochester on "The Inhumanity of Slavery."

1852 *Uncle Tom's Cabin* by Harriet Beecher Stowe is published.

1853 Frederick Douglass meets and talks with Harriet Beecher Stowe.

1854 The Republican party is formed.

1855 Frederick Douglass's book, *My Bondage and My Freedom,* is published.

1860 Frederick Douglass's youngest daughter, Annie, dies. Abraham Lincoln elected sixteenth president of the U.S. Carolina secedes from the Union in protest.

1861 The Confederates take Fort Sumter. The Civil War begins. Lincoln calls for militia to suppress Confederacy. The Confederates score a victory at Bull Run.

1862 Union forces capture Fort Henry, Roanoke Island, Fort Donelson, Jacksonville, and New Orleans. They are defeated at second battle of Bull Run and Fredericksburg. Lincoln issues Emancipation Proclamation effective January 1, 1863; all slaves held in rebelling territory are set free.

1863 Confederate victory at Chancellorsville, Virginia; defeats at Gettysburg and Vicksburg, Mississippi. Lincoln delivers the Gettysburg Address.

1864 Congress grants equal pay to black soldiers. General Ulysses S. Grant becomes commander-in-chief of Union armies. General William Sherman marches through Georgia. Abraham Lincoln reelected president of the U.S.

1865 Abraham Lincoln is assassinated. Confederate States of America formally surrenders at Appomattox Courthouse, April 9. Thirteenth Amendment to U.S. Constitution abolishes slavery.

1866 Fourteenth Amendment to U.S. Constitution prohibits voting discrimination, denies government office to certain Civil War rebels, and repudiates Confederate war debts.

1868 President Andrew Johnson is impeached for violating Tenure of Office Act, but is acquitted by Senate. U.S. Grant elected president.

1870 The Fifteenth Amendment, protecting blacks' right to vote, is passed.

1872 Grant is reelected president of the U.S. General Amnesty Act pardons most ex-Confederate soldiers.

1876 Frederick Douglass is the orator at the unveiling of the memorial to Abraham Lincoln in Washington, D.C. In a disputed election, Rutherford B. Hayes is finally elected nineteenth president of the U.S.

1877 Frederick Douglass is appointed marshal of the District of Columbia.

1882 First edition of *Life and Times of Frederick Douglass* is published.

1883 The Supreme Court declares the Civil Rights Act of 1875 unconstitutional.

1884 Frederick Douglass marries a white woman, Helen Pitts.

1889 Douglass is appointed consul general to Haiti.

1895 Frederick Douglass dies.

1964 Douglass's home in Anacostia Heights, Washington, D.C. is declared a National Monument on June 25.

INDEX- *Page numbers in boldface type indicate illustrations.*

135

ABOUT THE AUTHORS

Patricia and Fredrick McKissack, freelance writers and editors, are well-known authors of children's books, which include *The Civil Rights Movement in America* and the Start-Off stories produced by Childrens Press and the award-winning Christopher series. In 1985, the McKissacks won two C.S. Lewis Silver Awards for outstanding contribution in the area of children's literature for *It's the Truth, Christopher*, and *Abram, Abram, Where Are We Going?*

Other titles in the People of Distinction series written by Patricia McKissack include *Martin Luther King, Jr.: A Man to Remember, Mary McLeod Bethune: A Great American Educator*, and *Paul Laurence Dunbar: A Poet to Remember*.

The McKissacks, the parents of three sons, live in a large remodeled city house in St. Louis.